TAKE TIME
TO MAKE TIME
COUNT

TAKE TIME
TO MAKE TIME
COUNT

Karla C. Erickson

Bookcraft
Salt Lake City, Utah

Library of Congress Catalog Card Number: 84-72118
ISBN 0-88494-547-2

First Printing, 1984

Lithographed in the United States of America

To Barry, Jeff, Cori, Scott,
Kelli, Kacee, and Christy,
for the memories of yesterday
the joys of today
and the dreams of tomorrow

Contents

Take Time . . .

Time — that priceless commodity — seems to be diminishing in our busy, active lives. Do you recall sitting in your schoolroom, watching the seconds slowly tick into minutes while you eagerly waited for the bell to ring? How those minutes dragged. But now, looking back, how quickly the years have flown. Do you remember wishing away young years, dreaming of the day you could drive the car? The day you would graduate from high school and be independent? The day of your marriage? Just waiting for Christmas morning was agonizing. And yet, all too soon we hear ourselves say, "Where has the time gone? I never thought I would grow to be this old."

One of my most profound lessons was from a seminary teacher when he said, "What we do today will be our memories of tomorrow." At that moment, he urged us to recall our happy memories, then asked us to recall our bad memories. He pointed out that bad memories are usually regrets, and regret is a lonely companion. He cautioned us to use our time wisely in order to build warm memories, warning us that it takes planning and effort. In my mind I can still hear him say, "While you are in high school, make it the best time of your life. Accomplish your goals so that when you walk down the aisle for graduation, you will have no regrets, only good memories of the past years. Then, when you leave for college, or mission, or work, make *that* the best time of your life. Again, set your goals and be in charge. As you leave that part of your life and become a mate and a parent, again set your goals and be prepared to make the years of rearing a family the best years of your life."

Every day is a lifetime in miniature. If we could face every day with the intense realization that it is indeed a miniature lifetime, then we would learn to savor each day. Imagine the joy of one who can look back over his life and say, "I have lived 7,300 (or 21,900) miniature lifetimes and have enjoyed nearly every one."

Of course, no matter how we plan and work, not every day will be a bouquet of fresh flowers. We must remind ourselves that in order to enjoy the flowers, we need to plan for days of planting and watering.

However, no matter how dedicated we are to living each day to its fullest, concern for the future is natural. I called my brother on his fortieth birthday and asked, almost fearfully because I was also approaching that birthday anniversary, "How does it feel to be forty?"

Kent laughed. "It feels rather good," he replied. "When you can look back over your years and feel good about what you've done, then age doesn't really matter. I imagine it would be pretty sad to be forty and wish I could go back and change most of what has happened. Then I think growing older would be frightening."

Indeed, regret *is* a lonely companion.

In our present society, we are intensely aware of the number of years a person has lived. But instead of emphasizing the grandeur of aging with its positive points, we applaud the person who is forty and still appears to be twenty. Why are we so obsessed with appearing to be younger than our years? Are we living with more regrets than warm memories?

Trying to hide or camouflage our age is only a return to the years when we were children, dressing up in adult clothes, pretending to be older than we were. Unfortunately, as adults we are playing the game in reverse, with greater intensity. Sometimes we refuse to admit the truth, even to ourselves.

Now don't suppose that I feel comfortable with every wrinkle and gray hair. I, too, am flattered when someone says, "You don't look old enough to have six children." Secretly, I think I have fooled them. And that's exactly what I am doing—trying to deceive, to be artificial.

We cannot totally blame ourselves for falling into the trap. Society is engulfed with artificiality. The natural process of aging, as intended by our Heavenly Father, has been distorted with man-made artificial sweeteners. Of course, not everything man-made is bad or wrong. But in order to make each day a true fulfillment of time, we must not fill our minutes with artificial gratification, but rather we should concentrate on the long-term natural plan of God. Only then will we be at peace; time will be our friend instead of an enemy.

If time is to be an aid, it must be used in honest self-evaluation. Those moments are precious when an individual slips away alone and honestly evaluates his goals and actions. Taking time for private meditation is one way to determine whether or not artificial ways are smothering God's ways.

The current emphasis on optimum nutrition has sparked rebellion against artificial additives and preservatives in foods. But what about artificial additives in life? Surely they affect our souls, just as harmful food additives affect our bodies. Never before has society been so overstocked with artificial gimmicks "to make us happy." Yet, has there ever been a time of greater frustration and unrest?

We contemporary mothers are admonished to "take time for self-fulfillment." The irony is that *too many* classes, activities, and projects (intended to stimulate and improve our lives) destroy us with stress. The term "burnout" is indeed a household word.

Again, we must take time to evaluate what is real and what is artificial. Many of our activities build our egos for a short period, then leave us undernourished, much as artificial sweeteners cheat the body. Never has there been such a critical need for personal honesty in discovering our paths. When we reach ninety and recall today's social pressure and pretense, will we feel uncomfortable with some of our "miniature lifetimes"? Will we wish we could go back and change our lives?

Today's mothers live in a world which offers many options. Natural, God-given instinct urges a mother to rock her baby. But even more compelling at times is the current social pressure to "get out of the house; be all *you* can be." A young mother could easily become involved with too many other activities to the neglect of her family. As she rushes her babes to a sitter and discovers the sweet taste of the artificial additives, of course her spirits are soaring. But someday the artificial sweetness will wear thin, her babes will be grown, and her soul will not have had the natural nourishment which could have endured eternally.

The prophet, the Apostles, and other Church leaders tell us to go back to our homes, but society tells us that being home is not important. Elder A. Theodore Tuttle states, "Fathers and mothers are under divine instruction to take care of their parental responsibilities. The things we have done in past years are not now sufficient to protect our children in these critical times." ("Covenants, Ordinances, and Service," *Ensign,* May, 1984, p. 23.)

While he urges us to be even more conscientious parents, many of us are leaving our children more and more. We become involved in outside interests and activities, relegating the care of our little ones to sitters. We fill our calendars with trips and vacations, often leaving the children at home with a baby tender, telling ourselves that we will return happier and will, therefore, be better parents.

In reality we are relinquishing our responsibilities to someone else. Elder Gene R. Cook said, "Parents, whatever you are doing, *return home.*" ("Home and Family: A Divine Eternal Pattern," *Ensign,* May 1984, p. 32.)

Of course, if a mother finds it necessary to work for financial reasons, as happens so often these days, her minutes and hours at home must count.

For many years I have admired a mother of four who lost her husband when her children were still very young. Determined to remain self-sufficient, she somehow manages a full-time job along with her busy schedule of rearing her family. Late into the nights and long before the sun is up, her lights are burning as she wages her courageous battle with time and energy. On Saturday afternoons she probably would like to catch up on the cleaning and washing. Instead, she supports her daughters in their activities and her son in his sports. For example, she is the team representative for her boy's football team. At first she wondered whether she could find the time, but her son wanted her to be a part of his team and that was one way she could.

Such a mother teaches us many lessons. She does *not* feel guilty about working, because she and the Lord know there is no other way to be independent. She prays often, if not constantly, for the strength and energy and peace of mind to fulfill her many daily responsibilities.

When the Church leaders tell mothers to go back to their homes, they are speaking to mothers who do not need to work outside their homes for financial reasons. If the decision is made prayerfully and carefully, a mother who must work needn't feel guilty.

As we traveled out of state to visit my parents and

stopped in restaurants with our six children, we often felt the stares of other people. Our lanky teenagers first caught their attention, which usually shifted to our four-month-old Kristy.

For every meal, at least one smaller child was in a bad mood. Most onlookers would have questioned our "enjoyment." But children who are out of sorts are not limited to vacation times. Over the years I recall very few nights in which sleep was not disturbed by a child's bad dream or a baby needing attention. Plans for the day are interrupted by a sick child's demands, a phone call from an older one at school who forgot his report, or a myriad other shifts in my plans to help the children. Trips have been cancelled because of a sudden illness, shopping sprees shortened by a tired little one—the list could go on.

If parenting involves so many difficult times, why is being a parent a part of God's natural plan? Surely, the explanation is the concept of the price tag.

Early one Sunday morning as our family gathered in the chapel for sacrament meeting, we sensed a hallowed air. Our morning had not justified such a feeling; we had hurried and scurried frantically, yet had arrived barely on time. In fact, I had almost thought it better to stay home that day. But on the stand sat one of the newly appointed Apostles. Immediately we understood the reason for the special feeling. How grateful I was that we had not heeded my feelings and stayed at home!

A young departing missionary spoke at that meeting. He expressed his feelings of gratitude for his opportunity to serve the Lord. Then he said, "This is not convenient for me." He told how he had to juggle his affairs in order to accept his call and how much easier it would have been to decline, or at least wait a while. But he added, "When I think of the inconvenience, I recall the life of Christ. His life certainly was not to his convenience. It would have been much easier for him to take the road of least resistance. His death was most difficult to bear, both spiritually and physically; yet he remained committed to his calling."

I stood chastened. It had been inconvenient that morning to attend church. In fact, I could think of a host of things in the Church which are not convenient. Frequently, *children are not convenient.* Yet, as the new Apostle rose to speak, I felt a strong confirmation of truth, and once again I committed myself to my responsibilities.

I learned a lesson that day. If we had yielded to the convenience of staying at home, we would have missed that special missionary's message as well as the opportunity to hear an Apostle of the Lord. I needed to be reminded that if we parents do not commit ourselves to teach and train God's spirits, who will? The blessings of eternal life are not gained through convenience.

Everything of worth has a price tag. Inconvenience and setting aside one's own plans are a few of the price tags for those ethereal moments of cuddling a little one, the immeasurable pleasure of a late-night visit with an older son or daughter, the inestimable joy of a son or daughter's hug and kiss with the words, "I love you, Mom." Parenting is like any other career. If you desire to reach what you term success, you must pay the price.

God's way is often difficult. Struggling to teach and guide a frustrated child or searching for an answer to a prayer requires commitment and determination. Instead of choosing the easier way of taking an extended break during those difficult times, seek the Lord's help. Let him know of your desire to serve him by loving and guiding and teaching the spirits he entrusted to your care.

A mother who seeks to rear righteous children works directly with God in a common purpose—to prepare those children to carry forth his word. It is vital to realize that this is a once-in-a-lifetime opportunity and we must be willing to pay the price, knowing we will reap eternal blessings. We need to be careful even about our attitude when we feel like "taking a break" or "getting away." Is it because we are getting fed up with family members? We all talk about wanting to be an eternal family, but if we can't learn to live together happily on earth, how will we be able to do so in heaven?

Of course, there are times when I require private time away from the hustle and bustle of the children. But over the years I have discovered that what I initially termed "time to myself" was not easily defined. At first, I defined "time alone" as time with my friends, for truly friends are among the finest gifts in life, and time with them is important. I also used some of my limited free time to rush to the malls for shopping. However, I discovered that those hours away from the family did not revive my soul; I was searching for something more. I was, in fact, desiring time to *myself*. Instead of rushing out with neighbors and friends to various activities or scurrying to the store, I needed to find a quiet area and be alone with my thoughts. I needed time alone to arrange my schedules, to reestablish my priorities, to evaluate either progress or retrogression concerning my goals, to ponder, and simply to think.

My sister shares this thought: "I love to be with myself and my own thoughts because I always come away feeling good. I am nice to myself. Instead of belittling my ego, I try to build it and reassure myself that even though I need to try to do better, I am still an okay person."

My sister is far from being a hermit; her gregarious personality is attested to by her many friends. But she still takes time to be alone with her thoughts and to "be nice to herself."

In order to make time invaluable, we must clearly understand what our goals are. Consider for a moment some "great" people. Why were they remembered? Usually, they represent one area of high achievement. Emerson was a great philosopher; Steinbeck a writer; Mary, the mother of Christ. How do you want to be remembered? Now that there are so many opportunities and possibilities, you must answer that essential question for yourself. The answer can put you on target.

How will you make your time truly count?

I was visiting with a mother of eleven children. While she cuddled three little ones in her arms, she lamented the fact that she didn't have enough time in the day to accomplish all she desired. But when she was asked, "What is the greatest accomplishment you want to be remembered for?" without hesitation she replied, "More than anything I've always wanted a large family." Further comment was unnecessary. She realized that perhaps she was worrying about matters which held little relevance to her first priority.

Later she said, "After I came to grips with my real priorities, my days held more meaning. When I cleaned our home, bathed the children, or listened to them intently, I realized that I was actually building upon my greatest desire. Oh, I'm still frustrated when I'm around others discussing their projects and all the directions they're running in. Sometimes I forget my goals and begin to compare my days with theirs. Then I ask myself, 'What do I desire as my greatest accomplishment?' My actions are in focus again."

Not only is this mother touching the lives of her many children in a meaningful way, but she is also affecting those around her. As she teaches Beehive girls in her ward, she shares her wisdom through her lessons. One Sunday, for example, she taught a lesson on the scriptural phrase, "With an eye single to the glory of God." She asked the girls to insert the word "I" in place of "eye."

"Put yourself into the scriptures," she encouraged. "Then when you do even the simplest jobs, such as cleaning the sink or delivering the papers, if you do the job with an 'I' single to the glory of God, and if you try to serve with love, you will eventually come to fully understand the meaning of that scripture."

She then shared her own experience with the girls:

"Now as I put 'I' into that same scripture, my menial tasks assume greater meaning, for surely a mother serves. If I serve my family and husband with an 'I' single to the glory of God, then I begin to realize my worth."

Elder Marvin J. Ashton cautioned mothers against comparing themselves to others or pressuring themselves to become a "supermom" or "superwoman." He said:

"Some mothers seem to have the capacity and energy to make their children's clothes, bake, give piano lessons, go to Relief Society, teach Sunday School, and attend Parent-Teacher Association meetings. Others look upon them as models and feel inadequate and depressed and think they are failures when they make comparisons.

"We should not allow ourselves to be trapped into such damaging inferiority feelings. This is another tool of Satan. Sisters, do not allow yourselves to be made to feel inadequate or frustrated because you cannot do everything others seem to be accomplishing. Rather, each should assess her own situation, her own energy, and her own talents. Only you and your Father in Heaven know your needs, strengths, and desires. Around this knowledge your personal course must be charted and your choices made." ("Choose the Good Part," *Ensign,* May 1984, pp. 9-10.)

He urged women to set goals. "Without goals you can't measure your progress," he said. "Remind yourself that striving can be more important than arriving. If you are striving for excellence, if you are trying your best, day by day, with the wisest use of your time and energy to reach realistic goals, you are a success." Learn to *enjoy* the striving. Acknowledge the times when you climb another rung on the ladder of life. Savor the satisfaction of reaching just a little higher and catching hold of your goal. Deny yourself the easy shortcuts, the man-made artificial ways, and take time to make your time count— *eternally.*

Take Time to
Control Thoughts

Have you ever had a day when your thoughts were just plain ugly? Negativism sometimes creeps in from all corners to cloud the mind. On such a day you can find reason to be jealous of your neighbor, or your dear friend who never seems to have any problems, or your in-law who was promoted, or nearly anyone who crosses your path.

The more we allow ugly thoughts to take over, the more miserable life becomes. Why do we allow ourselves to wallow in self-pity? The secret word is "allow." Often I must scold myself out loud, saying, "This is absolutely ridiculous. I won't allow you to act this way." Those personal scolding sessions improve my focus.

One ugly trait which sometimes intrudes is jealousy, a deadly cancer which robs one of quality time. Several years ago, I had a conversation with my family in which I discussed the bad traits of a friend. In fact, I was actually demeaning her until Dad calmly said, "Karla, you are simply jealous of her." With flushed cheeks, I denied his accusation and ran to my bedroom. I hated to admit that my father was right. I *was* jealous of her.

Even now, when I find myself berating others, Dad's

comment comes to mind. I ask myself, "Are you trying to tear others down to make yourself feel better?"

Jealousy is one of those ugly vices which no one wants to admit. We want to be able to control such thoughts. Yet, in our affluent society of big homes, expensive cars, designer clothes, boats, recreational vehicles, and many other possessions, it is easy to covet what is not ours. Interacting socially with accomplished people sometimes leads to jealousy of their lifestyle. It seems easier to help people when they are suffering than to extend love and congratulations when they are successful.

Why is it so difficult to be sincerely happy about another's good fortune? Blessed is the person whose friends are sensitive to needs when ill fortune has crossed his path. Twice blessed is the person who has a friend who can sincerely exult with his good fortune.

I shall always hold dear those marvelous people who gave time and effort to help us through many difficult periods when I was expecting our babies. I spent a lot of time in bed, trying to keep the babies full term. Hearing the doorbell and smelling the aroma of hot, delicious meals for my family warmed my soul and taught me the blessing of charitable people. They taught me to love and to be sensitive to others' needs. To this very day I doubt if I ever expressed enough love to them; yet they touched my life and my family like no others. I needed their help.

On the other side of the coin, I remember the day that I received a call from an editor informing me that my first book had been accepted. I cried. I shouted. I didn't quite know how to handle the overwhelming joy. My first impulse was to share my joy. All was not as I had imagined; some friends could hardly muster congratulations. But others, bless their dear, loving souls, dropped everything at hand to join the celebration. That day is now a memory, and never again can I experience the same thrill of publishing for the first time in my life. But I cherish those marvelous people who could jubilantly share that day with me.

Whether it be producing a roadshow, sharing a child's joy in accomplishment, or the excitement of losing ten pounds, it is satisfying to have someone share that thrill. In order to share exuberance with a friend, however, our thoughts cannot be clouded with negativism.

But how does one rid his mind of ugly thoughts?

Perhaps that is one of the blessings of music. Two or three songs sung by our young children lift the blackest clouds from my mind. My ugly thoughts are quickly chased away by a child on each side of me on the piano bench, singing while I play. Or I love to turn on the stereo and play some of my favorite country/western music. Our older children often scoff when I turn on "cowboy" music and sing along at the top of my lungs. But I want them to remember that their mother loves western music; perhaps that will remind them of how much I cherish the memories of my younger days spent on a farm, surrounded by my horse and dogs. Music can be the springboard to memories, flooding the mind with warm, happy thoughts.

Another method of routing bad thoughts is to read something uplifting. Of course, you will want to read subject matter of interest to you; you also should choose challenging material at times in order to help you grow. You might try choosing from a recommended reading list — and there is nothing wrong with sometimes reading just for fun.

Of course, one could not go wrong in reading scriptures. Quite the contrary. One mother comments, "I don't understand how this happens, but every time I read the scriptures, I feel uplifted. Somehow my thoughts fall into proper perspective and life seems less muddled."

Another way to lift thoughts is to tackle a project. Activity is the best cure for depression. During the last several years, I have noted that those who seem to be on top emotionally are usually "project" people. Even though their needs and likes vary greatly, they always seem to have a project in process or near completion.

Try a "people project." If you wake up some day to a gray sky and a chill in the air, and your heart feels as gray as the day, try doing a "people project." Sit down on the floor with your children and talk with them about some of the people in their lives. Invariably a name surfaces of someone who needs you. If your energy level is as low as the overhanging clouds, create, with the children, a low-energy project which fits your capabilities, yet sparks high interest. Lose yourself in the sharing and caring of that individual. At the end of the day, you will feel useful and important.

Gather paper and colored markers and, while the children draw pictures for the selected person, write a letter sharing your thoughts, perhaps saying how your life is better because of your friendship. Tuck the children's pictures into the envelope and send it on its way. You will receive a lift for the day.

Even though writing a letter doesn't seem like much, it does carry weight. I have found that such a project reaps joyous rewards in my life when a return letter arrives a few days later. I am always astonished to learn how much that letter meant to the addressee at that particular time.

When physical and mental facilities are at their peak, imparting abundant energy, try a more ambitious people project. If negative thoughts creep into my mind, I think of someone whom I can surprise with an "I Care" gift. My little ones and I sometimes bake goodies. When abundant energy flows, the work of baking, cleaning up, and delivering the surprise is not overwhelming. In fact, I enjoy pushing myself a little harder. As I lift the babies in and out of the carrier seats and seatbelts, I realize that a great deal of strength is required for such efforts; I am grateful for high-powered days.

Learn to recognize your energy cycles. When you are "up," accomplish projects which require an extra push. When your energy level is "down," select people projects which are less demanding. As you might already have recognized, instead of saying "depressed days," I prefer to call them "low-energy days." Dwelling on the bleak word "depression" usually worsens situations. Thinking in terms of energy brightens the picture.

Few of us, of course, escape "low-energy" days. Those are times to put minds and bodies in low gear and slowly climb the rocky road. However, nothing is wrong with being in low gear. We can still experience positive feelings or newfound joys. Sometimes only low gear gets us to the top of the mountain, where the view is greatly broadened.

Another type of people project involves the everyday people who live under the same roof with you — your family. One day I found myself fighting to hold back the words, "No! No! No!" to little Kacee. Overnight she seemed to have turned into a destroying angel. Everything she touched was torn to shreds. She evacuated the cupboards, dumped the garbage out, and painted herself instead of coloring books. What to do?

One afternoon during this period, Barry called and, just as he asked how my day was going, I turned to see Kacee in our entranceway throwing shredded coconut into the air. By the time I grabbed her, the new package contained only a few bits of coconut and the maroon tile looked as though it had experienced its first snowstorm.

As I grabbed Kacee in my arms, Barry chuckled over the phone. "She does some of the funniest things. I hope you're keeping track of them," he said.

Those antics were not what I termed "cute," but his comment made me think seriously. I was so absorbed in the drudgery of cleaning up those messes that I was overlooking the whys and hows. An idea was born! Why not keep the camera close at hand? When the little girls made a mess, before the necessary cleanup I would snap pictures and compile a book entitled, "The Little Girls."

After my change of attitude, the next mess seemed only half as bad. Kacee was in the middle of cleaning out the pantry and Kelli was at her side. "Hold it, kids," I called as the camera flashed. They grinned from ear to ear. There was only one problem. They were misled by my enthusiasm and became more eager than ever to create another disaster. It took a little juggling of communicative skills before they understood that such antics were still taboo. Inevitably, the messes continued and the book grew. As I wrote about each little picture and tried to capture their childish capers and expressions, my love for those little characters increased.

The point is that even when stressful situations cannot be altered, changing your attitude can make them blessings in disguise. "The Little Girls" is now a treasure book. Never again will my daughters be exactly as they were on the days we snapped those pictures. But thank heaven for Barry's comment. Those priceless moments became a people project to be relived again and again; our little ones will have fun some day showing the book to their children and grandchildren.

I know what your next comment is. "But you have two little girls to share only one book!" There is method in my madness. I'm trying to build bonds—tangible bonds to endure after they are grown. On the back page of the book I have written a letter to both of them, sharing my reasoning behind the book. Then I have explained that as they have experienced these growing years together, I hope they will continue to share each other's lives, helping each other to learn and grow as they did when they were little girls. After they are married, the book will be given to both of them to be shared. Of course, the thought is idealistic, but in realistic terms, the book is tangible proof of a warm and loving relationship and perhaps—just perhaps—it will be a tool in keeping their relationship alive and growing.

Another suggestion for keeping negative thoughts at bay is to change the daily schedule. Instead of merely going through each day's normal schedule, change the routine and add spice. Call this project your Rainbow Week. Choose a particular week; divide it into "reasons for living"; color each day with a project with a purpose.

To begin with, the Sabbath is white—a fleecy white lining which starts and ends the colorful Rainbow Week. Make it a "Feeding your soul day." Read good books. Let your mind reach new spiritual heights. Attend Church meetings and glean everything possible from each person you talk with or listen to.

Color Monday bright yellow—"Love your home day." Devote your time and energy to creating something which reflects the love you feel for your home. Even if the project is nothing more than fresh flowers from the garden creatively arranged, savor each moment. Yellow is a cheerful color. Fill your project with that feeling.

One Yellow Day, for example, I glanced around our kitchen. Because it's the Grand Central Station of our home, it had lost its freshness. The little girls and I found fabric scraps to beautify large, empty peanut butter jars with lids. I cut out circles of fabric 1½" wider than the lids, then edged them with eyelet. Sewed-on narrow elastic gathered the material so that it fit the jar lids snugly. In one jar we put some cookies. Another jar became our sweet-tooth jar, partially filled with candies which had been hiding in my drawer for a special day. Another jar held peanuts. The kitchen reflected a bright, new appearance as we scrubbed floors and cupboards. I felt as cheerful as the jars.

On their return from school, the older children spied the jars, which received their enthusiastic approval. I knew that my Yellow project was a success.

Color Tuesday warm orange—"Warm thoughts and

actions day." A dear friend wrote recently and shared this thought: "I don't always work as quickly as I could because then the principles of kindness, patience, and understanding are lost for the sake of 'getting the job done.' It has taken me a long time to learn that lesson."

Wednesday is the "hump day" of the week. Color it red—"Create something exciting day." Prepare an innovative, fun dinner, or unusual after-school treats, or a surprise for the whole family. Let your children and husband know that you can also be fascinating. Do something ordinary in an extraordinary way. Life is as interesting as you decide to make it. Too often we tend to let the "doldrums person" dominate the home and our lives.

Color Thursday blue—"Learn all you can day." Because of mundane daily schedules and responsibilities, we forget that new, thrilling ideas are everywhere, waiting to be grasped. If you are fortunate enough to have little ones at home during the day, introduce them and yourself to a day of learning. Dust off the encyclopedias; re-explore the books you've bought for the children. We have a variety of ways in which to learn new things. Visit the planetarium, the zoo, or the art gallery and delight in *everything* you see and read. Thursday can become a favorite day.

Color Friday pink—"Personal improvement day." Take time to discover that neglected perfume or a new hairstyle; freshen or refurbish an old outfit. Teach your children the joy of taking time for personal grooming and development. Teach them about skin, hair, and nail care as you groom yourself. During the process, teach your girls to be girls and your boys to be boys.

Color Saturday green—a "Being together day." This is the culmination of your Rainbow Week. Plan a special family outing or gathering of which every family member will feel a part. Whether it be going to a football game together or a picnic to the mountains, include everyone.

As night falls and you all kneel in family prayer, your heart will be filled with joy as you look at each member of your family and recall your day together. What a perfect way to end your Rainbow—you have found your pot of gold!

Some might scoff and say, "What a silly idea to have a week of colors!" However, sometimes it takes an absolutely absurd idea to awaken us to the discovery of some finer things in life which we often overlook. It is in the tasting of these simple delicacies that our perspectives are heightened.

Of course, there are times when your physical condition is not good and a Rainbow Week might seem an impossible effort. Your health certainly affects your thinking. How do you lift your thoughts when your health is not at its best?

I learned how to handle this situation while I was pregnant with our sixth child. Barry opened the door after work one day wearing a grin. For months he had been working out with a health program and had been playing tennis consistently. I had noticed the gradual positive effect on his physical fitness.

"Hi, Honey," he grinned. "Well, I finally made it down to my lowest weight in years, and I feel great!"

At any other time I would have been equally exuberant. But I casually remarked, "That's great. Are you ready for dinner?"

Barry did not realize that instead of getting in better shape, *I* was noticing a protruding stomach. I also knew that because of previous problems, I would not be able to continue an exercise program. I would gain weight and become a blimp with no muscle tone. Early every morning, instead of running, I had to lie in bed perfectly still, because the slightest motion sent my stomach into a sea of nausea. I dreaded stirring up pancake batter and the aroma of oil heating on the grill. Instead of hugs and kisses as Barry rushed out for work, I could hardly muster a good-bye.

Inside, I was feeling sorry for myself, muttering that I wished my family could experience the nausea and discomfort in order to know how terrible it was. Losing my meals and feeling sick twenty-four hours a day continued. I dreaded the approaching Mother's Day because I did not want anyone to say anything nice about me. I felt that any praise was undeserved.

One late evening, while struggling to keep down my dinner, I suddenly turned to Barry and started to cry. "Honey, I feel so sick. I can't keep anything down. I hate getting fat. I'm worried that I'm too old to be having a baby." Just sharing my burden lifted the weight of the world. I had held my feelings back, not wanting Barry to think I was "weak."

Barry admitted that he could not fully comprehend my feelings. "But I'll do everything I can to help," he assured me. "Just let me know when you need me."

The following morning I was still nauseated. But somehow the gray clouds did not seem to hang so low. After hugging my three big kids and Barry on their way to school and work, I crawled back into bed with Kelli and Kacee and told them I needed to close my eyes for a little while. We three cuddled. As they looked at me with big brown eyes of concern, I realized how delightful it would be to have another little one come to live with us.

Instead of continuing to battle a tight, harried schedule, I rearranged my coming months, cancelling what I could. There were still the carpools for school and sports, but I tried to stay home as much as possible. I planned more reading time and singing time with the little girls. I scheduled more time for personal care to make sure I looked as good as possible in spite of my changing body size.

One morning after the 7:00 A.M. piano practice and breakfast, I crawled back into bed and little Kacee snuggled in beside me. She whispered, "Mommy, I love you." We lay there for long minutes, just visiting. Then I realized my blessing in disguise.

Had I not been at my low-energy time (pregnant), I would have been up and rushing, involved in an active daily schedule. I was now blessed with heavenly moments, in which time almost stood still. I vowed that each day I would seek out similar moments with each of our children and with Barry. After programming quiet moments into my life, I seemed to talk more slowly with the children, and I didn't feel the pressure of meeting so many deadlines. I found myself thinking of small ways to make our home more peaceful. I was amazed that what I had anticipated as nine months of gloom was turning out to be a growing experience — in more than one way.

I found more time to brush the little girls' hair, more time to work on projects for the children, more time to prepare good meals. Yes, there were still hectic moments when suddenly all the children had to be in different places at the same time. But hurried moments became the exception rather than the rule — a picture much different from what I had previously been painting.

One young mother shares this thought: "During the first two or three months of pregnancy, I don't understand why, but I am very emotional. I find myself either happy and carefree or sad and gloomy, as though the world weighs heavily on my shoulders. By the end of the third month, I usually begin to return to normal. But as bad as they seem, those first months are not all negative. That period gives me a chance to really consider my innermost thoughts and feelings and I know myself better."

I could empathize with her feelings. It was during those low-energy days that I viewed my marriage in retrospect. I recalled our early years when I taught high school and how much I loved my profession. But that was only the forerunner of what I was yet to discover. Barry and I became parents and that was the beginning of the most exciting adventure I had ever experienced. I recalled each child and the day of his or her birth. I recalled those years of watching little ones learn to crawl, to walk, to communicate.

I gave my time to teaching them, being with them.

Those memorable moments became indelibly imprinted on my mind. Barry grew in his profession, but his greatest growth came in his role of father. The number of his golf-playing days diminished as more children called him "Daddy." But for everything we gave up personally to be with our children, our rewards were magnified. True, each child brought new worries, new fears, and new traumatic experiences. But along with each child also came that unspeakable joy which parents feel as they struggle to teach and to guide.

For the remaining months of that pregnancy, I made sure that each day held meaning, no matter how miserable I felt. Our oldest son seemed to grow six inches in that time, and I found myself often staring at him, thinking how much I loved him. Never again would I be able to romp in the leaves with him as a little boy. But I am grateful that we took the time to play when he *was* small. Our teenage daughter also caught my eye frequently. I was almost startled to realize what a fine young woman she was becoming. Her many talents overwhelmed me. I liked what I saw. Never again would we sit in front of the mirror making silly faces while I fixed her long pony tails for Primary. But I was grateful that we had shared so much together while she was that cute, bouncy little girl.

During those months of pregnancy, I struggled to keep up with our busy Scott's athletic schedule. I cried as I watched Barry coach him throughout an exciting baseball year which took his team to first place in state. Following right behind baseball were those football Saturdays, watching Scott quarterback his first-place team. Often I hesitated to attend, but my doubts were erased as Scott hugged me after each game and said, "Thanks, Mom, for coming and watching me play ball."

When school started in the fall, the three oldest left each morning. As I watched Kelli, it was hard to imagine that the next year she, too, would be skipping out the door. In just four short years, we two had built a strong relationship. Looking into her face brought tears of joy. Actually, I dreaded the day she would leave for school, for she had become such a special companion and friend.

When I was a few weeks from the new baby's arrival, I found myself more and more attached to little Kacee. No longer would she be "my baby" and I knew she also sensed that fact. She always wanted to be with me. I loved brushing her pretty blond curls and dressing her in frilly dresses. I chuckled at her mischievous antics and empathized with her tender feelings. She would soon be the big sister to help Mom with the new baby.

And the baby—how does a woman grow to love a baby so much before she even arrives? At night I could not rest well, and I spent many early-morning hours contemplating life with my newborn. I loved to feel her move within me; every day and night I prayed for her safe delivery and good health.

No longer was I out speaking or doing the various things women my age usually do. But my days seemed more meaningful than ever. Perhaps I had to struggle with my thoughts in the beginning to know what makes life worthwhile—but during those months of struggle, I came to realize once again why we are here on earth. My deep love for Barry blossomed even more fully. I was grateful for his patience and understanding during that difficult period.

Whether pregnant or in the prime of good health, whether young or old, whether male or female, one of the traits of being in charge of one's life is being in charge of one's thoughts. Those who are in charge of their lives and thoughts are usually happy people. Surely they have come to realize the importance of taking the time to control thoughts. "Sixty seconds of bad thoughts robs us of one minute of happiness." And who does not wish for happiness?

Take Time for Creative Living

Ten A.M.! Usually by that hour our home is straight and I am spending time with our preschoolers. On this particular day I could not believe that the morning was almost gone and I still needed to fold clothes, clean fingerprints off the bottom half of the windows, and help little ones put away toys.

I glanced at my face in the mirror and all I could see were lines and wrinkles. "Falling apart at the seams" seemed an apt description.

I grabbed the vacuum and proceeded to clean up the orange-drink powder Kelli had accidentally spilled on the family room carpet. I mumbled, "Why even try? Nothing ever stays clean and straight." I didn't realize that I had an audience who was taking my martyrdom quite seriously.

"I'll help you, Mommy," said little Kelli, her big brown eyes full of empathy. "I can mop the entrance."

That's all it took. "I will help you" changed the picture. I vacuumed more quickly as I watched her mopping cheerfully.

"I'm all done," Kelli announced. "Mommy, I love you," she said, and we hugged.

Wrinkles—messy house—unfolded clothes—dinner waiting to be prepared—it wasn't really all that bad. I clutched Kelli's hand and turned to view our home. It didn't look that messy. In fact, it looked beautiful to me. The entrance tile sparkled in the sunlight. Kelli had done much more than scrub a floor. She had scrubbed my mind free of frivolous worries and troubles, which can cloud the true picture. As I ran past the mirror with baby Kacee in my arms, I laughed. Why, even those wrinkles didn't look quite so formidable.

Because we are often overwhelmed with daily concerns, the first effort in exploring imaginative ideas is difficult. Discouragement is often inevitable under the pressure of mountains of laundry, ironing, cooking, and cleaning. It's easy to fall into bed at night, exhausted, and wonder if it's all worth it. But once we cross the barrier of discouragement, our minds suddenly sparkle with originality. Exhilaration of discovery is indeed broadening and opens the door to other unfamiliar paths, even to self-discovery.

Turning home into a heavenly haven is not an easy task. However, it can be one of the most exciting challenges a woman faces. Begin with that fascinating individual—the mother. Of all the creatures on earth, she is most intriguing. She has within her grasp the means of transforming mundane moments into adventures. I admire the woman who can rise above menial tasks, which often sink the rest of us into the ground, and create memorable moments.

If anyone doubts the creative ability of women, he should visit any handicraft shop. Unique creations can grow from scraps of fabric, ribbon, weeds, or whatever. Teaching others and sharing discoveries and talents only increases the fun. Classes are available on just about any subject. Participation is stimulation. But be cautious! Attending too many classes can dull an individual's innate creativity. It becomes easier to depend on someone else rather than to discover an original new way. Some-times a person even loses confidence in her own creative powers and becomes bound to printed directions.

In order to make time really count in self-discovery, our inborn creativity must be challenged. Be daring in creating your own projects. Some ideas arise from need; some seem to float in the air just waiting to be grasped. At times you might become discouraged and feel like quitting—but don't give in to those whims. Creative thinking turns the ordinary into the extraordinary.

One fall, dried flower arrangements were "hot items." Since weeds are very expensive in craft stores, the chil-dren and I headed for the hills near our home. After filling two huge plastic bags with weeds, we gently placed them in the car trunk, leaving the lid open to prevent crushing our treasures. At home, armed with cans of various colors of spray paint, glue, a number of salvaged containers, and most of all *enthusiasm,* we created "flower" arrangements for our home.

It was fun tugging at the weeds to separate them and then placing them carefully in the vases. The back porch was transformed into a workshop within minutes. Some of the weeds we sprayed various colors; others we left natural. Making something completely original was thrill-ing. Of course there were moments in the process when I questioned whether it would turn out well. Undaunted, I kept working until the arrangements evolved into in-credibly attractive art pieces. The children applauded my endeavors. By late afternoon, four complete dried flower arrangements stood on our kitchen counter.

Although I knew they were not professional works of art, I was surprised that I could do so well without any instruction. With every new piece, I learned more and my self-confidence soared. Sometimes, when I was tempted to discard my work, forcing myself to keep going resulted in one of my better creations.

That first night when Barry arrived home for dinner, he was obviously a bit disturbed as he glanced at the backyard strewn with weeds and debris. He had worked diligently to keep it neat. "Oh, Honey," he gasped. "What are all those weeds doing in the yard?"

I tried to reassure him that everything was under control and soon those weeds would be gorgeous arrangements. Then I showed him my works of art. Even though he was unconvinced, he confessed that he liked our "masterpieces." Our home certainly radiated a homey touch. But the real thrill came when visitors asked where we had purchased our "lovely arrangements."

I do not share this experience boastfully. Believe me, not all the arrangements were spectacular. But I had learned a lesson. If all that creative power to make weeds into arrangements was just waiting to be ignited, then possibly there were other areas that had never been tapped. By experiencing the surge of creative thinking, I understood the wise person who said that we do not use even one-tenth of our potential power.

I realize that some readers will immediately say, "That's fine for her. But I don't have creative genes."

The more people I know, the more I realize the potential of human beings. Not everyone would discover the satisfaction I did in turning weeds into decorations. But everyone I know seems to possess some unique trait which could easily be a launching pad to the discovery of his own creative thinking. Then, after once discovering that potential, a person can use formal instruction as a springboard to greater achievement.

A young mother who is well-known for her artistry was upset. After teaching herself the simple lines of calligraphy, she took a class from a renowned teacher to improve her skill, then developed her own ability by extensive practice. Of course, the more she practiced, the better she became. But she said, "I'm surprised how many people just want to copy my patterns. Why don't they learn the basics from me, then create their own style so that their efforts can be a reflection of themselves?"

The work of artists mirrors their feelings and emotions. Similarly, many people experience a great satisfaction in decorating their homes with creative projects which reflect their personalities. Fluffy pillows, rugs, tablecloths and centerpieces, wall hangings, and furniture are only a few ways of integrating our creations into our homes. The more *you* are reflected in your home, the more you love being there.

Remember to include your children in your plans. If your creative additions lend added personal warmth to your surroundings, the same could be true with your children. Encourage them to select their own wallpaper or to create items which can be displayed in their rooms. With some encouragement from you, their rooms could become their havens.

Creative ideas maintain enthusiasm.

Mid-May! And snow swirled outside. Instead of little sunsuits, I bundled the girls in warm, snuggly sweaters. Gray clouds outside seemed to dampen our spirits. The older children were at school. Barry was at work. And the three of us were at home, needing a "lift in life."

Mustering enthusiasm, I asked the girls if they would like to help me clean the house, promising a surprise when finished. As usual, the word *surprise* caught their attention. Immediately we were folding clothes and dusting shelves. We worked quickly in anticipation of that surprise. When the last bundle of clothes had been tucked away in dresser drawers, we hurried to "Mom's Store."

When we had built our new home, we had included a guest room so that visitors would not feel embarrassed by pushing some of the children out of their beds. The guest room soon became my room for special gifts and displays. Soon the children started calling it my store. Whenever they needed a gift for a birthday party, instead of hurrying downtown, they always asked if they could go shopping in my "store" (which is stocked with gift items purchased on sale).

That snowy day, from the closet of my store, I brought out two wrapped boxes, one for each little girl. Several months previously, I had spotted two little dresses on sale. Since I knew the girls would be needing new Sunday dresses, I had them gift wrapped, then put them away. As Kelli and Kacee giggled and squealed while opening their gifts, the color of the day changed. Those packages certainly had given them a "lift in life"!

But what about Mom? Hidden in a corner was a gift with my name on it. When I pulled it out, the girls squealed again and could hardly wait for me to open it. The box contained towels for the bathroom. They were simply gorgeous.

Whenever I go shopping, I am always looking for basic needs for the children, whether it be socks, jeans, underclothes, or a new shirt or dress for church. No matter what I purchase, I buy it for a "lift in life" gift. If the store has wrapping service, I have it wrapped there. But if not, then I take the purchase home and wrap it immediately, always marking for whom it is intended. As I mentioned, I even gift wrap household items, such as the towels. Mothers need "lift in life" gifts as much as children. It's amazing how a pretty package to Mom can brighten a dreary day, even if she knows what's in the package.

When I sense that someone in the family needs a "lift in life," I pull out a brightly wrapped gift and wish that person a happy day. Whether it's a new pair of socks or a set of new barrettes, just the fact that it was wrapped as a gift seems to work magic.

Be creative. There are so many practical things which

must be purchased for a home and for everyday needs. Why not spice up life and give those practical necessities —even toothpaste and toothbrushes—as gifts?

Of course, the secret is to keep the gifts tucked away for a surprise. Don't give just to be giving. If the occasions are widely spaced, the children do not come to expect them. If handled wisely, this idea can be a teaching tool for children to give to others to brighten lives.

We have a huge basket in our family room which is the "gift basket," filled with gifts for loved ones the year around. Even our children visit it occasionally to see if their names are written on some of the packages awaiting their birthdays, for example. Pretty packages adorned with bows are an attractive decoration in any home which almost intimates that there is a party around the corner.

Whether a party is planned or not, every day should have a purpose. Purposeful days lend meaning to life. For example, on Tuesdays the little ones and I dress up for our shopping day. Summer months find our school kids going with us on our shopping jaunts. Sometimes we just window-shop or browse; on other shopping days, we carry a shopping list. This special day provides a perfect time to teach personal grooming, clothing care, and similar concepts. We scurry to complete all our housework early in order to have the day together. I take extra time to brush their hair and tie bows. And when we are shopping, we enjoy every minute at leisure. Once we are ready, we board the Bronco and are off, singing at the top of our lungs.

Often they spot items which they want. This is a perfect time to explain methods of *wise* shopping.

Another day is designated as "writing day." I explain to my preschoolers that Mom would like to spend a few hours in the den at the typewriter. I am usually fortunate if I manage to complete a paragraph for the day. But there are many other types of writing which we do on that day, also. There are always letters to write to grandparents, and scrapbooks and photo albums which need updating. It is a perfect time to teach them about journals.

One inexpensive but thoughtful idea for writing day was shared by a dear friend. Whenever she discovers an article about someone she knows, she always clips it and encloses it with a letter to that person. To help preserve the article for her friend's scrapbook, she uses clear plastic shelf paper to protect the newsprint.

Whether it be writing a letter to a friend or a member of my family, or penning a simple thank-you, my writing day always proves to be worthwhile. Even though the day flies, at its end I can account for at least one important accomplishment.

Take the time to create purposes for each day of the week, such as a Rainbow Week (described in Chapter 2). Even investing only part of a day provides a sense of accomplishment.

Another way to change the mundane to the spectacular is by changing your feelings about yourself. Again, be creative. I shall always recall the day Barry phoned with his exciting news. After our marriage, he had joined an accounting firm. One of his long-range goals was to someday become a partner in that firm. He knew the road would be difficult. As the years passed, the time arrived for his name to be considered. For months we had been waiting for the decision. At 1:10 P.M. I received his call. His first words were, "We're in, Honey, we're in." But instead of shouting it to the rooftops, his voice was filled with gratitude and humility.

This was an unforgettable day in both of our lives— especially in Barry's, because one of his dreams had materialized.

As I hung up the phone, I mused, "A partner." My baby was fussing and as I gathered her into my arms, I thought, "A partner in an established national firm! Barry has achieved one of the highest goals which he set for himself many years ago. Am I accomplishing any of my long-range goals?"

Questions crowded into my mind. Would I ever experience the joy of success which Barry felt? Could being a mother at home, with crying and fussy babies, provide a similar feeling of achievement? Would Barry outgrow me while I remained at home rearing children and keeping house? I had heard of many marriages which gradually dissolved because the husband outgrew his wife and their paths separated.

All the time that I was experiencing feelings of joy for Barry's accomplishment, it seemed that I was also experiencing worries for what it might mean to our marriage.

And then it struck me. Just to have the name "partner" sitting on the desk or inscribed on the door does not guarantee a sense of importance. I could be just as professional as I desired. The whole secret of success is to realize the importance of one's work. Perhaps I needed to know that my work was just as vital as even a top executive's.

Self-evaluation followed. When I think of a "professional," I think of someone who is constantly alert to improving his work. He is aware of innovations in his field. He is equipped with necessary equipment for proficient work. He *knows* that his work is important.

Were my working conditions on that professional level? My first thought was, "I do need a better can opener and more efficient drawer dividers." That sounds so ordinary. Yet I had to start somewhere. I next checked to see if I had enough cleaning supplies in various parts of the house to prevent needless running. I started to make necessary lists.

Then I attacked the schedule of the day. Was I wisely utilizing those early minutes right after breakfast before the older children ran off to school? If each of them did just one task, it would be a boost to my chores. Of course, an executive does not spend an entire day straightening his desk or arranging his papers; he quickly completes the mundane tasks in order to tackle important problems. I knew I must come to grips with my motherhood goals.

For me, working with those people within our four walls carries the greatest importance. I felt that I must organize so that limited time would be spent on the menial, yet necessary tasks, leaving the majority of the day free to invest with Barry and our children.

I found myself laughing out loud at my new sense of authority. I liked being a "partner." Then the truth dawned. Barry and I are the "partners" in charge of our home. We actually are like partners in our own firm. We agree on goals; we hold our weekly discussions on financial affairs; and we consistently, if not constantly, are helping each other to be aware of those "employed" in our own little firm. Just as the manager is given more authority, I recognized that we had just promoted Jeff to a manager in our firm when we had given him more responsibility as well as more freedom.

Each time we welcomed a new arrival, it was like hiring another employee who needed teaching and training.

Our family home evenings could be likened to a weekly firm meeting with everyone attending to discuss goals, ideals, and plans for the coming week.

Suddenly our little firm held much more importance than any large national corporation. Those whom we employed would never be fired. They are brought into the firm with the intent of each becoming a partner in his own firm. Even if personalities clash, ways of maintaining compatibility are discovered. The partners feel responsible for the growth and development of every member of the establishment.

In our firm, the whole individual is considered. We

take time to play together, to study together, to work together, to pray together. We cannot afford to dissolve our
firm; our goals and aspirations extend into the eternities.

After realizing my partnership status, I could understand why Barry's voice was humble on the telephone. I,
too, felt grateful and humble to be one of the partners of
the Erickson firm. No longer did I question the importance
of my status as "partner in charge of home." Viewing my
role as professional sharpened my once-fuzzy focus, for
the feeling of being a professional motivates one toward
constant improvement.

In trying to improve our time, we naturally consider
the term "organized." But organizing is not an easy feat.
Often an evening which is scheduled for family relaxation
turns into pandemonium as we hustle to gather materials
and information for a report which is due the following day
for one of the children. There are constantly unscheduled
necessities occurring after school and, even if I have every
minute organized on paper, it is unrealistic as well as frus-
trating to fight the realities. Often there is a vast difference
between being organized and making time count.

The secret is in establishing priorities. Instead of being
a person who is superbly organized, I would rather be
classified as a wife and mother who can take the time for
whatever she feels is most important.

Can you guess who taught me this valuable lesson?
It was (and still is) our children. Many times when my
schedule was organized, when our home was organized,
and when my thoughts were organized, one of our children
became ill. Before I knew what happened, he had thrown
up all over the freshly-laundered linens and he needed
some loving. Suddenly my organization exploded. These
are moments when priorities take over and I must make
my time count. The little hug, the tender words, the
rocking made my time count.

Anyone walking into our home at such a time could
very well think that I am anything but organized at 4:30 in

the afternoon with bed linen soaking on the counter, waiting to be washed, and toys strewn about by a two-year-old still scattered while I tend the baby. One might even think I'm lazy to see me rocking the baby, surrounded by such chaos. But if our time is to really count, we must not let the remarks of others disturb us. What really counts is the inner assurance that all is well. In fact, it has been during some of those hectic moments, when our home looked like a hurricane disaster, that I have made my time count the most.

In our contemporary society, women are urged to succeed in almost every area. Constantly we are admonished to get out of our homes and find the "real me." However, the exciting adventure of self-discovery requires wisdom. While you have small children at home you may need to let the creative juices flow and find crazy, fun ways at home not only to find yourself, but also to let your family know what an interesting person you really are.

A few summers ago, when our family was caught up in the craze of physical fitness, Barry bought me a backpack and warned that I had better get in shape because our family was going backpacking. "In shape," I muttered. "Of course I'm in shape. Why, very few women can hustle through a grocery store as quickly as I, and I do run up and down the stairs all day long." I fooled no one, not even myself; I did need to work on physical fitness. But with my time demands, how could I possibly go to the spa to firm up toneless muscles? I did not want to be left on the trail as Barry and the children waved good-bye. What could I do?

An idea popped into mind. I loved the feeling of being ahead in my housework. I decided to set my timer for thirty minutes and, instead of doing the daily chores at my usual pace, I would jog through each room. I had read that the best way to build heart stamina is to jog. So I jogged and cleaned at the same time. For the first time in months, I did not scowl when I noticed the children had not taken their clean clothes from the laundry room to their drawers. Those clothes gave me a reason to run up and down the stairs countless times. I was off. First the laundry room, to the boys' rooms, back to the laundry room, and on to our daughters' rooms.

Fortunately, the first time I was trying out this new idea our two little girls were involved in Sesame Street and their toys, so I jogged and jogged and jogged. As I polished the mirrors, I jogged. As I shook rugs, I jogged. As I scrubbed fingerprints off the wall, I jogged. When my two-year-old walked into the kitchen and needed a glass of juice, I took the glass from the cupboard, poured the juice, and handed it to her, all the time maintaining my jogging pace.

She looked up at me, puzzled. "What hurts, Mommy?" I started to laugh so hard that I had to take a minute's break.

"Mommy doesn't hurt," I reassured her. "I'm just jogging while I do some of my work. I'm going to be in great physical shape."

As she walked back into the family room, she kept turning around to look at me jogging while I put the orange juice pitcher back into the refrigerator.

When baby Kacee started to cry, I vacuumed with one hand and held her with the other arm, all the time jogging. She seemed to like the new ride because she smiled and giggled and waved her arms in the air. Again, I found myself laughing out loud and thinking how absurd this this must look if anyone were to peek in.

Thirty minutes. The timer buzzed. My reddened cheeks and my perspiring face proved that I had certainly exerted myself. My legs felt a little weak and I needed to catch my breath. But how light my heart felt! Not only was the vacuuming completed, the kitchen cleaned, and a batch of washing done, but I had also completed my physical fitness workout for the day. Hooray! I figured I was hours ahead of the usual day's activities.

It is sound advice to keep in good physical shape, even if backpacking trips are not the goal. (Incidentally, the backpacking trip was great fun and my jogging paid off.) You can live a more creative life when you have the energy that comes with physical well-being. But let's not think solely of "our" needs and "our" activities, forgetting a major reason for the project in the first place: our physical appearance should be at its best for the people we love most—husband and children. We should be excited to maintain top physical fitness in order to have more stamina and strength for activities within the four walls of home. It would be easy to forget the total picture and become too involved in the "me" syndrome. Once that happens, even formerly worthwhile projects can become detrimental.

Another worthwhile project which lends itself to self-discovery and all the time maintains the correct order of priorities is creating warm memory reminders for our children. Some of my warmest memories are wrapped around two people whom I dearly loved—my grandfather and grandmother. They had been like second parents to me, and my young life was intertwined with their memories. Upon their deaths, I longed for a memento. In their basement I found an old pot which they had used in the mountains at their sheep camp. After cleaning it, I spray-painted the pot black and tole-painted a picture on one side. Today it holds plants in my home—and pleasant memories.

Mother saved one of Grandmother's favorite hats. I carefully stored it in a hatbox. Even now, many years later, when I take the hatbox down, I fondly recall the lady who wore it. That hat posesses intrinsic value. No price tag can be put on an article which warms the soul with memories of one who has touched your life in a unique way.

Nearly every home claims a clock which triggers memories, even if it is only the memory of waiting for the school bus. We have such a clock in our home. Many times when I listen to the chimes, I am reminded of previous

minutes passing. Since I feel it important to share my feelings about that clock, I wrote a note and slipped it inside
the case. The note reads:

> "To one of our special children who will receive
> this clock: May you always recall the many good times
> we have shared as a family. Think fondly of our young
> years in baseball, football, and drill team. Recall all
> our fishing trips to Island Park and our backpacking
> excursions.
>
> "May the chimes bring a soft, flowing peace
> throughout your home much as they did in ours. May
> the chimes always remind you that even though the
> minutes, hours, days, and years might pass quickly,
> someday we will all be together again, where time is
> endless.
>
> Lovingly yours,
Mom and Dad"

I am intrigued by a particular woman who can show
guests through her home, relating unique stories behind
every belonging. She taught me to use better judgment in
acquisitions. She taught me the importance of displaying
meaning in our lives. Otherwise, objects take over, and
both the mind and the house become cluttered and
confused.

Another lady tells how she bought a teddy bear for her
two-month-old son. She watched her child, as he grew,
carrying his teddy from room to room. When he outgrew
his favorite toy, alive with memories, she gave the bear an
important chair in their living room. She laughs as she
explains, "Not everyone has a teddy bear in their living
room. But then, not everyone has a teddy bear which
means so much."

Portraits of family members are priceless. They depict
what is most important to a family. Throughout our home,
the walls hold picture groupings which remind us of the

year Barry and I were engaged, backpacking trips together, and the many stages of our family's growth. In order to give added warmth, many of the frames have been handmade to blend with the decor.

Taking the time to give purpose and meaning to a few of our special belongings pushes out the artificiality of material things. Of course, I am not saying that we never buy anything new. But once again I was reminded of what life is all about when we were expecting our sixth baby, and I had decided that we needed a new fancy wooden cradle.

One evening my sister visited, and in her car trunk was our much-used bassinet which my brother had used for his baby. That bassinet had held each of our babies, as well as many of the cousins on both sides of our families. Memories flooded my mind as I recalled our children being laid in it as newborns. The following day, the little ones and I scrubbed the white paint to a gloss. They were fascinated as I told them stories about that bassinet. We bought fabric to make a skirt and sheet. My heart was full as we tied ribbons and placed the finished bassinet in a prominent place, awaiting our new arrival. I had come dangerously close to disposing of something which was filled with warm memories.

Much as you might take inventory for security purposes, take inventory of your belongings and decide which pieces hold special memories. Then take the time to share some of your thoughts with your children. Dining tables are often special places where a family gathers as they not only share the food to nourish their bodies, but also share ideas and thoughts to nourish the soul. Write a note and slip it under one of the leaves of the table where it will be discovered someday when that same table is given to one of your children. Big, comfortable chairs which have been stuffed with memories, rockers which have been used to settle a little one's cries, dishes which have been handed down from grandparents—anything that radiates good memories should be inventoried and restored with added dimension.

By taking time to preserve warm memories, we will help to fulfill our children's natural need for belonging and being loved. Whether it be in building a memory, jogging in the home, creating a unique wall hanging, or doing a simple puzzle with a child, projects within the home can be most stimulating and exciting. And remember your calling as the partner in charge of your home. *You* are important! *Your status* is important!

Establish a strong partnership with your mate, and then take more time to teach and train those little employees. When you call upon the principal partner in charge, your Heavenly Father, for his counsel, surely he will guide you in making your time on earth count toward eternal goals.

Take Time for the Holidays

Ah, the holidays! Our progenitors were wise in establishing holidays for relaxation and a change of pace.

In bleak February, when the glamour of white snow has faded into gray and black puddles of slush, we eagerly await spring. And suddenly Valentine's Day is upon us. Plan ahead for this holiday. When school supplies are on sale in the fall, that's the time to purchase extra glue, white and colored paper, and other necessary items. Then in February you will be ready to create some lovely home-made valentines.

At our home, Valentine's Days are special because cousins deliver a plate of heart-shaped cookies, personalized with our names. Not only are the cookies delicious, but they also add a special warmth to the day because they were made just for us. It doesn't matter what you do, as long as it's something traditional, such as mailing cards or delivering them on doorsteps, then running and hiding after ringing the bell.

Easter is the time to teach children about the Resurrection and our relationship to our Savior. No matter how many times that story is retold, it holds greater meaning with each added year and each telling.

Easter time also holds the fun of the Easter bunny. Instead of hurrying the children off to attend organized egg hunts, try planning your own and enjoying the squeals of delight right at home.

After we were married, I discovered that one of Barry's favorite projects is coloring Easter eggs. As the years passed, our traditions evolved. The day before Easter finds all of us gathered around the kitchen counter with cups of colored water and boiled eggs waiting to be transformed into works of art. There are the usual solid colors with transfers of ducks, flowers, and other designs. But then there are the daring ones with designs in purples, browns, blacks, and yellow. That evening the eggs are stacked in a huge bowl and left for the Easter bunny to hide after he fills the children's baskets. Early in the morning, Barry and I are awakened with squeals and laughter as the children have their own egg hunt throughout the house.

Creating traditions makes holidays memorable. Plans need not be elaborate, but should be structured for the entire family's enjoyment.

For example, there's the Fourth of July. Some families traditionally attend the annual parade; others simply have a picnic in a significant place. Traditions sometimes evolve. A wise parent notes the events which the whole family enjoys then lets them become an annual affair.

A few years ago, we purchased a pack of fireworks. Since aunts and uncles and cousins decided to meet at Grandpa and Grandma's for a picnic, we brought our fireworks along. Thus began the tradition of the annual fireworks display in Grandpa's backyard. Each year rekindles memories of the past and new memories are perpetuated. Now the families, old and young, eagerly await the Fourth of July.

One Halloween the children and I created a huge black

spider with huge googly yellow eyes. To set the stage, we used black crepe paper and made a net which hung in one corner by the fireplace, the spider in the center. Alongside the net we hung the pumpkins, witches, and goblins, which the older children had made in their school classes. During the month of October we certainly had a spooky, delightful corner in our home.

As another Halloween approached, I wanted to create a fresh centerpiece. My first impulse was to visit the hobby shop and examine displays. But I had a brainstorm instead. Why not delve into drawers, cupboards, and closets and rediscover some old treasures which might be incorporated into a decoration? I began a search of the house.

In one cupboard was a big porcelain orange pumpkin with black eyes and mouth which a dear friend had made for us years ago. As I lifted it down, a flood of warm memories of that loved person swept over me. In one corner of a closet I discovered some dark bamboo mats which Mother and I had purchased on one of her visits. I recalled with pleasure that enjoyable day spent in the mall with Mother and Dad. In my ribbon basket I found the right color and texture of streamers. With the addition of dried weeds, my project was in full swing.

Next I spotted three brass ducks, a birthday gift from a dear sister-in-law. Brass polish restored the luster; again I was reminded of the day that special person gave them to me.

My centerpiece grew into a treasure of memories. The huge orange pumpkin sitting on the bamboo mat became the focal point, the dried weeds and ribbon adding a decorator touch. The three shiny brass ducks were scattered between weeds and ribbon. My counter glowed with the new decoration, but it was the warm feeling inside which assured me that we needn't rush to the store to purchase craft pieces. After the family had all gone to bed, I ran downstairs to savor my new masterpiece.

Decorations for any holiday do not have to be elaborate. Whether it be an Easter basket on the counter with after-school treats or green streamers for St. Patrick's Day in a corner of the family room, taking the time to create something tells family members that you care enough to make the extra effort.

Why not bake holiday cookies together? One clever mother is always looking for unusual cookie cutters. For each holiday she doubles or triples her standard cookie dough recipe, then she and her children cut and design festive cookies.

One afternoon they invited Kelli and Kacee to share in their cookie day. Several hours later our little girls returned home, each carrying a plate of cookies in the shapes of hands, armadillos, ice cream cones, and dinosaurs. The little girls' expressions reflected their fun and excitement. Our friend found a warm spot in their hearts with the warm cookies. She will remain one of their favorite people because she gave them much more than cookies; she created lasting memories. And sent them home on a plate.

Lately I have heard too many mothers state that they never bake goodies any more because they also eat and gain weight. But in the histories of forefathers/mothers and loved ones, note how many references are made to their mother's cooking and the resulting good feelings. When one recalls the sighs and smells of home, blessed are they who can recall with fondness that warm, yummy sensation which accompanies goodies as they come from a toasty oven. Each holiday merits a good baking day spent with Mom in the kitchen. Not all baked goods must be crammed with sugar. As mothers know, baking and decorating means a messy counter and sometimes a dirty oven to clean. But worthwhile memories usually require effort.

One of the secrets of enjoying any holiday is preplanning and organization. List on paper your desires for that holiday. For Halloween, for example, you might want children to remember certain enjoyable activities shared with the family, and so on through the year.

Several years ago, I felt that our children were not experiencing the real significance of Thanksgiving. In spite of the traditional family meal with cousins, aunts, uncles, and grandparents, something was lacking. One year, on the evening of November first, we each told of one thing for which we were thankful. Out of white posterboard I made a calendar, listing each name, then added twenty-six spaces across the poster. We explained that by Thanksgiving Day twenty-six items for which we were thankful would be listed after each name, climaxed by the annual Thanksgiving dinner.

Kelli was just past a year then. Many evenings we burst into laughter as she told what she was grateful for. She was on a kick of liking peas and for many evenings she always said she was thankful for peas. Family bonds were cemented as we realized how grateful we were to be a family who could laugh together.

Again, with planning, one week before Thanksgiving Day I took out sheets of parchment paper and, with the help of stick-on letters styled in calligraphy, I created documents for each person, noting their thankful items. At the bottom was added: _(Jeff Erickson)_ , having given thanks for the above items, is entitled to attend the annual Thanksgiving feast.

(Signed by Mother and Father) _____

_____

Thanksgiving morning, we presented the certificates, concluding a simple but significant project. Each evening, as we had recorded something for which we were thankful, we had been reminded of what is truly important in life.

Of course, the annual highlight is Christmas, which demands planning and organizing.

Christmas is like a huge feast, anticipated all year long. Imagine a gigantic smorgasbord. As far as you can see, the table is spread with all kinds of food, any one of which could be a delicious treat. So it is with the holiday season. There is much to do, many places to go, and many people to see—and each event could be memorable. But too often at the feast, we grab the largest plate we can find and try to fill it with everything, only to discover that we have overstuffed ourselves.

During the holiday season, why not forget tasting every available event? By limiting what we put on our plates of activities, we can save some of the delicacies for future years. Instead of gorging, why not savor what we do taste? And lest we forget, simple occasions are as refreshing to our souls as is a glass of ice water to the thirsty.

Then there is the problem of overextending our means with gift purchases. We hear our children talking about all the new toys they want. Here again, in hopes of a grand feast, we pile our plates with bills and more bills, leaving us in agony. After the holidays, we are left with more bills than memories.

One parent explains her dilemma thus: "As Christmas nears, I become almost weary just thinking about all the activities I must attend and presents I must buy. As I recall last Christmas, I think of all the gifts under the tree, and how the kids counted their presents to see who had more. Our calendar was stuffed with parties and festivities, some of which I really didn't want to attend.

"This Christmas must be different. But how do I change the pattern? I wish we could take a trip where we could forget the whole thing and concentrate on being a family together. Perhaps we could use the money normally spent on gifts to buy our tickets."

The more she thought, the more she realized that not always can we run away from a situation. But that doesn't mean we can't change what we don't like. One of life's blessings is each new day with its opportunity for change.

After much contemplation, this family realized they did not want to leave home for the holidays. Instead, they decided to trim their Christmas. They trimmed the Santa list, they trimmed their activities, they trimmed expenses and made as many gifts as possible. What they added to their Christmas budget was *time*. They wanted to take more time for the simple family traditions which meant the most to them.

A father says, "Our most treasured Christmases include more of our family traditions. I like to recall, for instance, the evenings we decorate our tree and pop the corn and thread it on string to make ropes."

Another parent adds, "I'll always remember Christmastime when I was a little girl. In our town lived an older lady who each year invited us neighborhood children to her home and asked us to bring a quarter. We practiced and practiced, preparing a program. When it was ready, we took the quarters and bought a cake or pie, then hurried off to a shut-in or an older person who seldom had guests. Following our presentation, we left treats. We loved to see their faces light up with smiles. That made my Christmas!

"Now that I'm older," she continues, "I wish my children could have experienced that thrill with our dear neighbor. Years later, I suddenly decided to be that kind of lady to the children in our neighborhood. This past summer I gathered the nearby children and my own and we created a dazzling program which we took to rest homes and to bedridden people. It was an exciting time! And now that the holidays are nearing, I'm doing the same with them for Thanksgiving and for Christmas."

In order for time to count at Christmas, list what means the most. One mother stated that most of all, she wants to maintain a peaceful feeling in her home during the holidays. "I accomplish this by having nearly all my shopping done by November 30. On the first of December I begin to celebrate with the family. We wrap gifts, make baskets of fruit for families, and deliver them together. My husband and I schedule few evening activities to take us away from home. We are together more as a family and we try to teach our children that giving to and thinking of others is what Christmas is all about."

So this Christmas season, list on paper what is important for you. For example:

Homemade cookies which the kids can decorate

Homemade gifts for special people
Homemade candies
Homemade decorations for the home
Stories shared with the family
Gifts for each special person
Christmas cards
Decorating the tree

Give each item a priority for a different day. This speeds up the daily routine tasks. Making lists simplifies the otherwise overwhelming burden of Christmas preparations. On the days set aside for gift wrapping, take time to reflect on pleasant memories of the person whose gifts you are wrapping. From Thanksgiving dinner to Christmas dinner there are thirty days over which to spread creative preparations. By not crowding everything into a few days, there is time to savor the creative fun.

Whether you're hanging stockings or placing wreaths on the doors, listen to Christmas carols playing in the background. If you have little ones at home, let them be a part of the events. Share with them your feelings about your home and let them experience your enthusiasm as you decorate.

By making a list, you eliminate unimportant items because you can see in black and white how much you want to do and how much time you have. In this way, you can handle unexpected incidents in stride.

I think the most memorable Christmas we shared as a family was the Christmas we gave it away. We had moved into a new home which we had planned for years, and had just experienced the birth of a new daughter. Our cup was running over.

As Barry gathered us together one evening during the first week in December, he mentioned our many blessings. Then he asked, "Is there anything you really need?"

"No, not really," said Jeff. "But there are a few things I'd sure like."

"Oh, yes," joined in Scott. "I'd like a new pair of roller skates."

Cori sat deep in thought and little Kelli squirmed in my arms.

"Since we need little, would you like to give your Christmas to someone else?" Barry asked.

The idea stunned the kids.

Barry continued, "I know you would like a gift from Santa." The children laughed. "Maybe he can find one small surprise for each of you. But the biggest part of your Christmas you would give to someone you don't even know."

He then turned to me and asked me to share with them what I had discovered about a certain family. I didn't know their names, but from a friend I had heard of their dire circumstances. They had suffered extremely high hospital bills, and just when they needed money the most, the father had been laid off work.

At that point, interest was high. We all decided that we would keep our project anonymous. Barry and I had the name and address (which was some distance away) so we could deliver the gifts. For the children to truly experience giving anonymously, they would not know the names; however, they would go with us to deliver.

The following week, we enjoyed making our boxes of love, filled with clothes and gifts for each of "our family's" children. We went shopping one evening for oranges, apples, and toys. By their contagious enthusiasm, one would have thought our children were buying presents for themselves.

Delivery night finally arrived. Boxes were piled high, but our excitement was even higher. On a card we explained that they didn't know us and we didn't know them, but we wanted to share our Christmas. Then Barry took out a crisp, green bill. The kids' eyes really lit up when they realized the amount.

"Can I feel it?" asked Jeff. "I've never seen one of those before." I must admit that even I was surprised.

"You see, kids, when we decided to give our Christmas away, that's just what you're doing," Barry explained. "This money would have been buying some of your gifts. And those gifts which we bought for them might have been yours."

The room was quiet. "I just hope I didn't give them my roller skates," Scott said seriously. We all broke into laughter, but we were ready to deliver.

The crisp night air reflected our electrical excitement as we loaded the gifts and boxes into the Bronco. Nearing our destination, we suddenly became quiet and tense, for the home was dark. We had not considered the possibility that perhaps "our family" could be gone for the evening. Before enthusiasm could waver, Barry quickly asked who would like a treat. We were off to the nearest drive-in. We drove back again, but still no lights.

"Let's drive around and look at the decorations," Barry suggested. We drove all over our town, gazing at the festive decorations. But none of the lights brought the joy we felt as we drove past "our family's" home and saw lights on.

Barry pulled the Bronco about halfway up the block. Once again we were tense.

"Honey," I said, "I think you're shaking."

Barry laughed. "I am," he replied. "I've never done this before."

"I sure hope they don't have a big dog," said Cori.

"Okay, Jeff, you carry this box," Barry instructed as he organized the delivery. "Scott, you take this one. Cori can take these toys and I'll carry the others. Jeff, you stay at the door until we've all put our packages on the steps. Put this Christmas card on top and ring the doorbell, then run like crazy. I'll have the Bronco running and we can pull out before they even open the door."

Everything went like clockwork. As they raced back to the Bronco and we took off, we have never experienced that same excitement which seemed to make us all feel airborne even though our Bronco was on the pavement. That evening, during family prayer, our hearts were full and we each felt that we had already enjoyed our Christmas for that year.

Christmas Eve found Barry and me most concerned. As we laid out the scanty Christmas, we feared that perhaps the children would be disappointed in the morning. I searched the drawers to see if there wasn't something else to put out.

Early on Christmas morning, the kids raced to our bedrooms to have our family prayer before we all hurried to the family room. Our principal thought was, "We hope our family is having a great Christmas."

Barry's and my fears of the previous evening were unfounded. Though gifts were limited, love was abundant. We took more time than in previous years to open gifts from each other. Each gift was truly appreciated.

That year we all began keeping our personal journals. It was a joy for the children to write in their own words about Christmas. One of them wrote, "It was the best Christmas I've ever had. I hope we do it again next year."

How we chuckled as Scott wrote, "It was great! And I even got my roller skates."

Barry and I learned a lesson. We expected our children to be disappointed. However, the project proved that the real meaning of Christmas is diminished by too many toys or games.

Of course, this is not something every family would want to do. Every family is unique and can discover their own unique joys. Most important is to take the time to savor the holidays. In so doing, the Christmas spirit will remain alive in vivid memories throughout the coming years.

Take Time for Those Frustrating Finances

One of the dilemmas which will plague most of us at some time in our lives is "survival of money mania." Usually we enter marriage with little experience in the field of money management. However, once we exchange vows, we are expected to become financiers immediately. Fortunately, most of us begin with little and usually (we hope) our knowledge grows with our income.

The ideas in this chapter do not offer suggestions for making a million, but rather how to live on what you make.

Throughout our seventeen years of marriage, we have encountered a few embarrassing moments concerning money. By our sharing some of our blunders, perhaps some of you might benefit. As you read the accounts, you will most likely recognize bloopers much more quickly than we did.

I shall never forget the evening we phoned my father and told him about our prospects of an exceptional investment. We asked if he would trust us with a loan which we could repay within six months—interest and all!

"What's the investment?" Dad queried.

"Oh, we can't say a word," I replied. "The promoter told us it must be kept strictly confidential because it's on ground level. We just know we're going to make a mint."

Dad was somewhat reluctant. However, assuming we possessed some common sense, he lent us the money. We plunged into our first big investment. Soap!

When a truckload of the product arrived at the doorstep of our tiny apartment, we were overwhelmed with the amount of our purchase. Marketing the product was much more difficult than we anticipated. Barry was involved with his new profession and I was loaded with responsibilities as a teacher. The first cold fact hit—neither of us felt comfortable about selling the product.

Our manager sensed our frustration. To lift our spirits (we thought), he told us that he had made a deal to sell some of our soap to his clients out of state. As he loaded his trailer with half our inventory, we were relieved. But our tension mounted once again when he cautioned, "Don't take this check to the bank yet. I must receive payment for the product first. I'll let you know when the check can be cashed."

That was the beginning of a terrible nightmare. For days we held the check, awaiting his phone call. Inside, I sensed we had been taken for a ride, but my optimism prevailed as I convinced myself that our friends would never cheat us. Having that check in hand was proof that everything was aboveboard.

Finally, in desperation, we took the check to the bank. A few days later it came back stamped "Insufficient Funds." We frantically located our manager. His cheery voice dissolved some of the fears. He told us to return the check to the bank for immediate cash. I scolded myself for doubting. Again, the check went to the bank—and bounced!

This continued for several weeks. Finally, when we could not reach our manager by phone or mail, we admitted that we had been swindled. Not only were we left with a check that bounced, but half our inventory was gone. We sold some of the soap and made enough to pay back part of the loan. Barry and I could hardly face my father.

Red-faced, I expressed our embarrassment to Dad. He didn't react with the expected gasp of disbelief. Instead, he wisely told us: "If an investment has to be kept secret, even from those who lend you the money, that's usually the first indication all is not right. If the deal sounds foolproof, hesitate. Remember, anyone who has a foolproof deal, guaranteed to bring in high returns, would not give away the idea to others. I've learned that the higher the return, the higher the risk."

Dad continued to remind me of our home life and how he had made his success one step at a time: precept upon precept, hard work upon hard work. He continued, "Don't go into debt to make a quick dollar. Earn your way in life honestly by doing a good day's work. Life doesn't owe you a living."

And then to soften our hard blow, he added, "Use this as a learning experience. Be grateful that all was not lost. Always remember your big soap deal when another hot investment tempts you." Then he grinned. "I, too, had to learn the hard way. My deal was with vitamins!"

Stories about exceptional investments are rampant. Granted, there are those who know the investment field and are trained or have the knowledge to build their fortunes with wise investments—but people seldom share stories of how they lost their money. Our shelves, still loaded with soap, continue to remind us of our naivete.

Many are eager to tell you how to spend your money. Remember to let your head make the decision—not your heart, and not your friends. Take time to consider the investment from every possible angle. Ask yourself, "Can I really afford it?" Not only are you investing current cash, but you are also investing the interest which that cash could accrue.

Before taking your hard-earned money and investing in something you know little about, *stop!* Take the time to consider the results if your deal falls flat. We knew little about selling or marketing soap. Perhaps if we had invested more time in learning about the situation, we would have known that we had no business in that kind of venture. If we had figured out how long it would take us to earn that much money (without borrowing), we would not have been so eager to jump into the slippery deal.

However, investments are not the only culprit in mismanaging financial affairs. A family must learn how to keep everyday expenses within their income. Since each family's income is as varied as each family's needs, learn how to live within *your* income in order to survive money mania.

For example, when you are broke, even the smallest amount of money is important and you are grateful for it. But you may become discontented when you compare your situation with that of others who are earning more. I advise you to forget other people's incomes. Treat your income as a personal matter, much as you do your underwear. No one needs to see it or hear about it.

If you happen to earn a modest raise, consider it a blessing. Don't be concerned if others earned a larger wage increase and are spending more than you. Everyone has enough problems with managing his own affairs without trying to worry about someone else's financial situation.

Attack your finances as an exciting challenge. *Make out a budget.* List the necessary monthly expenses. By listing your payment to the Lord first, you are immediately reminded of the true source of your income. Next, pay yourself—including putting some into savings—even though it be a modest amount, to learn the gratification of earning something for yourself. Third, list necessities such as mortgage, food, and utilities.

Fourth, list insurance, dentist, doctors, and similar expenses, and know when they are due in order to allot the necessary funds. If you are fortunate enough to have some money left over, put some in "miscellaneous" in order to sidetrack those unscheduled disasters which usually interfere with planned expenses.

A mother at home who does not bring in an income still needs money. She should not have to account for every penny, except to herself, if she so desires. Some husbands forget that a wise woman at home, doing the family's cooking from scratch, the washing and ironing, the housecleaning, and all the household duties, often saves more money than if she left each day for a job and had to hire those services. Her value is increased in the face of the combined costs of babytending, work clothes, transportation, and eating out.

Husbands, if you are fortunate to have a wife who can run the family affairs on a tight yet livable budget, take the time to express your gratitude. Let her know that you appreciate her efforts and her results. Be sure to recognize the long-range blessings of having her at home with the children. She might be saving future money which would be spent on counseling or special schools for children whose self-esteem never surfaced because no one was there when needed. No one can affect the life of a child quite like a mother who discovers joy in teaching and guiding those special spirits.

Many times money could be saved if parents recognized that they are a prime source for teaching skills as well as principles. I was impressed when observing a large family who has recognized this fact. They pay for the older children to take music lessons; when they become proficient, the older children teach the younger. Not only is money being saved, but familial ties are being strengthened. In years to come, those younger children who become adults and enjoy their talents will recall a brother or sister or mother or father as the prime instructor. But in our fast-paced society, parents are sometimes reluctant to take time for those teaching responsibilities because we feel our time is too limited. So we work harder to make more money to pay someone else to give their time to our children. Don't misunderstand me, I am not against lessons for children. But whenever I have substituted myself for the teacher of our children, we have all received bounteous blessings.

One example relates to our two little preschoolers. I determined to teach them myself, even though I had not received training in that area. But I was their mother, and who else cares for their growth or well-being more than I? That was my qualification, along with my enthusiasm for the project. Together we shared glorious moments. One morning after we had worked on our letters and sounds, we spied ripe bananas on the kitchen counter. "Would you like to learn how to make banana bread?" I asked them. Their squeals of delight answered my question and we quickly collected flour, sugar, and other ingredients.

Monetarily, consider our results. We had homemade banana bread for dinner, at a savings over the commercial product. I saved a day's preschool tuition for two, plus gas for travel.

But the greatest asset far outweighed the monetary consideration. My pay came when Kelli looked at me with sparkling eyes and said, "I love you to be my teacher, Mom." To see them proudly serve "their" bread to the family for dinner was an experience money could not buy. They had enjoyed learning at home; now they watch eagerly for bananas to ripen.

However, in order to keep our learning at home fun and exciting, I do have some expenses. I watch for clearance sales, such as the after-Halloween sales when costumes are reduced seventy-five percent or more. For two dollars we had costumes which are still being used for make-believe time. I also watch for the school sales to pick up crayons, markers, and paper for the year ahead. For their birthdays I watch for puzzles, books, and other items for learning experiences.

While children are still young, we should anticipate

the days of missions, college, and marriage. Those are expensive items which require wise planning. Let the children know why you save for those coming years. Let them be a part of the saving program. Take time to share with them ways in which *they* can save for a mission or schooling. By doing so, they are broadening their visions. Explain the need for constant saving so their goals can someday materialize. When the day does arrive, take the time to verbally remind them how their prudent saving and self-denial of frivolous spending is responsible for their current comfortable circumstances.

Take your children shopping with you. Let them see the price tags on clothing. Children are never too young to realize that money should not be squandered.

As mentioned previously, Tuesday is our shopping day. After the older children have left for school, we get dressed up for an exciting day. The little ones and I drive to the mall or a small local store, depending on current needs. One afternoon we drove to the shopping mall about twenty miles away. On the way we sang our usual songs and enjoyed chatting and visiting. I told them that bathroom rugs were on sale. (Sometimes I'm sure they equate my enthusiasm with the word "sale.")

As we hurried past the children's department to the housewares, Kelli spied some frilly pink dresses.

"Oh, Mommy," she cried. "Look at these pretty dresses." She grabbed one off the low-standing rack and held it up to her, exclaiming, "It's gor-geous!" (a new word in her vocabulary). "Oh, Mommy, can I have it?" she pleaded.

My heart said yes. My head said be cautious.

I enthusiastically told her what good taste she has and how much I liked the color. "Let's look at the rest of the dresses," I suggested. We spent a while studying the entire rack. Kacee decided she wanted a new dress, too. When Kelli ran back to the original pink dress, Kacee grabbed one, also.

"Now we can both have a dress just alike," squealed Kelli.

I held up each dress to their faces, envisioning them both running to church in those frilly frocks. However, they already had Sunday dresses.

"Girls," I said, drawing them both close to me. "Let's not buy these pretty dresses but keep them as our dream dresses. You don't want to always buy everything that's beautiful. Leave some things on the rack and just dream about them."

Without a sign of objection, Kacee wriggled out of my arms and ran to the stuffed animals. With a grin Kelli said, "Okay, Mom." She skipped off to join Kacee.

Of course, I don't believe in depriving children. But in our society, it is easy to give too much simply because there is so much to acquire.

The bathroom rugs were not the right size or color. We did, however, find shirts for Scott on sale. On our way home I asked the girls, "Won't that be fun to give Scotty his new shirt?" They cheerfully agreed.

The girls learned a valuable lesson that day. We had seen many things for them, but the package they took home was for Scott. And they were cheerful about it, inside and out. They seemed content with the time we had spent together and with their dreams of the pretty, frilly pink dresses. People spend too much on too many wants. Too many joys remain undiscovered because of too many material possessions.

Learning the difference between needs and wants is a valuable lesson for children—and adults. Such lessons take time, repetition, and determination, but are valuable to the members of every generation.

How can a large family survive financially today on a limited income? One fine example is a family with seven children. When I asked the wife how she and her husband survive so well, she replied, "We were both raised on a farm and we experienced the satisfaction of growing what food we need. We were not accustomed to luxuries, so we could be very happy with little. Oh, sometimes I thought how nice it would be to have things, such as a boat for our family to enjoy. Then we were invited to go boating all day with some of our friends. Our little ones were upset; they wanted to play on the beach in the sand, and found the boat confining. I decided that a boat would only get in the way of some of our simple and inexpensive pleasures."

She continued, "When I was only nine years old, my mother died and I helped Dad with the cooking and housekeeping. I remember thinking then that the only luxury I ever really wanted was an electric stove; I was so weary of carrying wood in for our stove every day.

"When I married, I did get an electric stove and even a dishwasher. Four years ago our dishwasher broke and needed replacement. But instead of buying a new one, we had other priorities. Our older children were interested in dancing and gymnastics. At first, we didn't think outside activities were all that important for children because they have so many opportunities at school. But when our daughter tried out for the school dance team, she didn't have the necessary background to become a member. Instead of buying the dishwasher, we enrolled her in dance classes. The following year she earned the right to be a member of the team.

"Through experience, we learned that it's important to provide means for our children to involve themselves in some extracurricular activity, not necessarily because it will help them provide a better living, but because it builds their self-esteem. We can easily wash our dishes, but building self-confidence is not as easy.

"Because we've never had a lot of extra money, my husband does most of the home, appliance, and car repairs himself. We have developed the philosophy that since someone else made these conveniences, why can't we fix them ourselves?

"I guess the only time I'm a little down is when I sense that other people think we can't afford anything. But I just have to push those thoughts out of my mind and remember that for *our* family, we're doing just fine.

"We have a garden and raise all our potatoes, peas, beans, and carrots. We have cherry and peach trees, so we only have to purchase pears, apples, and corn in the fall. We buy whole milk and mix powdered milk with it. I still do a great deal of sewing. But I have also discovered that when I sew, I am not only saving money but also achieving. It's that feeling of accomplishment which keeps me happy and moving ahead. Oh, there are times when I dream about all the fun we could have if we had lots of money, but interestingly, I am very happy with our life the way it is.

"Instead of saving money for 'things,' for us or for our home, we save for missions, weddings, and school for our children. Our oldest daughter, who is married, confided that she and her husband are determined to pay their full tithe even though it means sacrificing. She has a strong testimony concerning tithing and knows that her family will be blessed, as our family has been, if they keep that commandment. She realizes that one of the blessings is that they will always have plenty—perhaps not plenty of money to buy luxuries, but plenty of what they will need to get by on."

When I think of a budget, I think of the word self-denial, certainly one of the prerequisites of self-control. Self-control is a virtue which helps us understand more fully our reason for being on earth. Living on a budget can be challenging and exciting. Being able to live on less builds confidence. We often purchase items which clutter more than enhance our lives, thereby diminishing self-control. The more you buy, the more you want to buy. In this way you can easily wreck your budget.

Not relying on buying "things" to supply life's excitement puts a person in tune with more important matters.

If we can teach our children self-denial in worldly belong-ings, it is easier for them to comprehend the higher law of self-denial and obedience concerning temptations. Mas-tering self-control permits true freedom.

A dear friend suffered many difficulties. As a young girl, she was showered with clothes, new cars, and all the spending money she wanted. She married young because she was determined to have the one she "wanted." After several years, they were divorced and she struggled to obtain an education so she could support her children. She confided, "All my life I was accustomed to having what I wanted. I equated gifts from my parents with proof of their love. When I married, I was devastated when my husband would not give me everything I wanted. Times were tough, and yet I could not understand why he would not buy me everything. I took his actions to indicate that he did not love me. Bitterness surfaced and we separated."

In an article entitled, "The Poor Little Rich Child," Dr. Elliot Landau stated, "Few children can survive the curse of parents who give them everything. . . . We need to remember that our children are not made better, their character is not increased, by a surfeit of riches." (*Deseret News,* May 2, 1973.)

My father told us children while we were all at home, "I won't give you a lot of unnecessary things, but I will help you obtain an education because that's one thing which will help you become a better person."

He kept his word. Each one of us children graduated from college. Our playroom had few toys; he denied us the "frills," but he provided the means for learning.

I was intrigued with the comments from our stake patriarch's wife concerning the early years of rearing their children. With several small ones at home, they had little money to live on. Therefore, she could not buy things to make their lives more interesting. In fact, she couldn't afford a sitter, so she stayed at home with her babies.

"A blessing in disguise," she said. Instead of leaving them with a sitter, she utilized the few books they had, including the scriptures, and shared hours reading to and being with them.

Now that her children are married, she is reaping the benefits of those early days. A letter from her married daughter stated how she appreciates the warm memories of her mother rocking her while reading the scriptures aloud. She acknowledges that her deep love of the scriptures is a result of those many hours in her mother's arms.

"Going without" certainly can be a blessing. Restraint teaches us that too often what we consider necessary for happiness is nothing more than clutter to our minds.

Never be ashamed to live on a budget. In fact, deem it a virtue to choose to live on one. In our society of instant gratification, geared toward the buy-now-and-pay-later concept, turn the tables. The real joy of struggling to save for something important leads to appreciation, whether it be in the child who struggles to save for a bike or an adult who saves for a new couch.

This might sound absolutely absurd, but if you want to add zest and zing to a dull month, cut your budget and challenge yourself to live on less. It's an exciting project. It sharpens the mind. Even if you are "rolling in dough," challenge yourself.

Remember, handling finances should be personal, and the priorities of each family should determine the budget. Make a budget and discover joy in living within it. Teach your children the satisfaction of spending their earned money wisely and determining the difference between needs and wants. I recall the twelve-year-old girl who was asked by her father, "Honey, what do you need for your birthday?"

"I really don't *need* anything, Dad." Then with a twinkle in her eye, she added, "But there's a lot I *want*."

Take Time for Your Mate

During a luncheon conversation someone asked the question, "If you were on a sinking ship with your family and had time to save only one person, whom would you save?"

The majority of the women immediately said, "My children, of course."

Only one said, "My husband." She commented, "I would first save my husband, and together we would try to save the children."

Together. How many times is that word forgotten when it concerns the roles of husband and wife? Too often the husband's work takes him away for extended periods of time during the day. In many marriages, the children and house keep the wife busy—a situation which can result in husband and wife going their separate ways. If only couples were wise enough to realize that two working together are stronger than one. Whether it be three in the morning or six at night, take time to sit down together and visit about those things which are important to you both.

"One day I looked at my husband and gasped," a young wife related. "He was not the same man I married twelve years ago. What had I done to him?"

She continued, "When we were newlyweds, I knew I had married one of the greatest guys alive. He was not only good-looking and attractive, but he had a charisma which magnetized people. I loved going places with him and we shared many fun and exciting times.

"We were thrilled about our first baby, but that must have been when we started going our own ways, even though we didn't recognize what was happening. More children arrived through the years, and so I began pursuing my former career in order to provide more of the luxuries we wanted. I don't know how or when, but somewhere along the road of marriage, my thoughts changed, turning inward to myself, *my* career, and *my* needs. I had pushed my husband, as well as the children, out of my mind as much as possible.

"Many times I lay in bed in the mornings and let the older children fix their own breakfast of cold cereal. If they didn't have breakfast, I rationalized that it didn't matter. They should be capable of caring for themselves. I never even thought about the good-bye hugs or warm wishes for a good day at school.

"Oh, I did get up early enough to fix breakfast for my little one who went to kindergarten. But it was always the same—cold cereal.

"Since I had *my* career, I also had *my* money and I let my husband know which money was mine! I managed it, but not very well because often I could not account for the expenditures.

"I usually prepared Sunday dinner, but that was about the only time we were together as a family. After all, the kids had hot lunch at school. I went my way, my husband went his, and the children more or less floated around trying to find their way.

"Often I found myself thinking that the only way out of such a rotten situation was divorce. I could understand why so many women wanted out. But thank heaven for some sound judgment which came unexpectedly. One day I read a part of a book which talked about the importance of being together as a family. Suddenly I realized I was giving up what life was all about. If you do not share love with those close to you, what do you have?

"That evening I looked at my husband, who was no longer the happy, energetic man I married. I wanted to cry out and say how sorry I was for what I had done to him. It was really difficult to even try to talk to him—we had not communicated in such a long time. But clumsily I tried to explain my feelings. I tried to let him know that somehow I wanted to make up for all those years I had not been a part of his life, nor he a part of mine.

"Beginning was the hardest. The first move was to arise early in the mornings and fix the family's breakfast. I cut some of the hours I spent on my career and forced myself to think about the needs of my husband and our children. I even prepared evening meals. My kids were really shocked with their 'new' mom. One evening I wrote little notes to each one and tucked them under their dinner plates. I could not believe their excitement over such simple gestures from me.

"My heart ached that I had let so many valuable years slip away, and I shuddered to think I had come so close to losing them. But within I knew that it was not too late to try to become the kind of wife and mother I wanted to be. It was like a new awakening. It was so good to see my husband smile at me once again.

"Right now I am still trying to do all those little things which I should have been doing all along. I often find myself feeling much the same way as when I first met my husband. I have come to love him all over again. But this time, I won't let us fall apart."

Wives, remember the sentimental cards tucked under the windshield wiper, the little love notes, and the tasty surprises—your means of setting the trap?

Husbands, remember the flutters you felt when she first held your hand? Remember the flowers you sent, the love notes you used to bait your trap?

Over many years, why do we forget how important and meaningful those "bait" devices were? True, we are no longer young kids whose main objective is "catching" each other. Children have broadened our horizons, and with them have arisen a multiplicity of concerns and worries which cloud our minds. We also have responsibilities for house payments, jobs, and bills to pay—concerns which realistically keep us occupied.

But what about each other? I recall one morning when, for some unexplained reason, I had to be rated as a number-one grouch. Barry kissed me good-bye, and even that irritated me. That evening I was still the same miserable person. As usual, when I am out of sorts, it affects the entire family. That evening I was cold and ornery with Barry. Automatically, he became the same way. The vicious circle was in motion. The next morning he left without even a kiss. Isn't it bewildering how husband-and-wife arguments can begin without even a spoken disagreement?

That evening Barry cornered me and said, "I honestly don't know what's wrong. But I do know that when you and I are angry with each other, I can't do my work well, nor can I concentrate. So let's sit down and work this thing out."

The truth was that I, too, was not functioning well. I was feeling the pressure of letting Barry down as his wife. I felt guilty because I was not being a good mother, either. But when we sat down and talked about the situation, I tried to explain that I could not account for my bad disposition which had started the whole affair. It gave me the chance to hear myself say, "I don't know why I was so ornery that morning. I really wasn't mad at you, or the kids. I was tired. That's really my only explanation. But when you became upset with me, then I became upset with you, and it led to that rotten day for both of us."

In black and white, the entire situation reads like a joke. But how many times are our disagreements and arguments started on such a flimsy basis? Anyone could tell from reading this account that Barry and I needed to sit down and talk together.

It is highly embarrassing to admit that I caused a silly, unnecessary argument. But when it comes to the solution, why is it often difficult to sit down and talk with one another? Why is it so difficult to admit fault? Being married is not easy. But without struggle we would not scale the possible heights of joy. The harder a couple works at their marriage, the greater is the reward.

Attending one of Dr. Victor Cline's lectures, I was intrigued with his statement that men would probably never be able to fully understand the needs of their wives and vice versa because men and women are so different in their physical makeup. But it is in trying to understand, through compassion and love, that the relationship is strengthened.

When there is a need for mothers to work, husbands and wives rush out the door, leaving home problems behind. Certainly in these cases there should be a mutual understanding and cooperation for both husband and wife to share home duties. However, when husbands leave for work all dressed up to face the day, it is difficult for them to understand how their stay-at-home wives can be preparing breakfast and running around getting the kids off to school and not even be dressed. Sometime during the day, the wife does take time to bathe, dress, and even put on makeup. But about three o'clock her life is caught up in a whirlwind. By 6:30 her husband walks through the door, expecting to see a clean house, happy children, and an exuberant wife all waiting to heal his work wounds. Instead, he is often aghast at the situation. In no way can the wife fully explain her afternoon of carpools, gymnastic lessons, ball practice, and church meetings. Even though she is only one person, she is required to fill the role of many. Therefore, she feels lucky if dinner is on the table when her husband arrives from work. Thoughts of combing her hair may not strike again until the next day when the older kids have left for school.

As for the husbands, they leave the household problems with their wives as they walk out the door. But there is a mountain of obligations, pressure, and decisions awaiting them on the job. The day wears on their nerves, and they hope for quiet evenings and good meals as their salvation for the day. On returning home, they might find the family room cluttered with toys and the table not even set. One of the kids tells him that Mom is down at the church for a play practice with two of the other children. "What a disaster!" muses the husband.

Marriage requires a great deal of patience and understanding, even when one does not feel like it. Perhaps we will never quite appreciate each other's needs as we should, but with effort and determination, we can at least try.

One of the best ways to combat marriage fatigue is to start setting the bait traps again. The discovery will be that now it can be even more fun. You are more relaxed and the love you feel for your husband should be deeper. But how do you initiate such an idea?

Select one day each week and surprise each other with a treat or gift. Let the kids know what is going on. They soon anticipate those days, also.

Barry and I selected Thursday as *our* day for surprises. When we first started, I made sure to mark those days on the calendar for fear of forgetting. But now our surprise day provides my motivation to be more aware of Barry's wishes. I listen more intently to what he says because I am continually searching for clues to his wants and needs.

One Thursday evening Barry walked in the door and the look in his eyes told the story—he had forgotten. As he went upstairs to where his gift was all wrapped and waiting for him, I was uneasy. I didn't want him to feel guilty about forgetting. He came downstairs carrying his gift and gave me a hug, but he didn't say a word about his surprise for me. Later that evening, there on my pillow was a note which read, "I was so busy at work today. Sorry. This entitles you to a long, long back rub."

Another incident occurred during his busy season, when we are fortunate to see him at all. I know that he is busy; yet, that evening he came home swinging a bag of licorice for my Thursday surprise. "This isn't much, Honey," he apologized.

"Oh, yes, it is. You know how I love licorice," I replied. "And it shows you were thinking about me."

Choose your own day and have fun surprising each other. This little project seems to help you tune in to each other. Whether a bag of licorice, an expensive gift, or a gift of service, the most exciting part is that you are thinking about each other and that you care.

Another bonus is the picture your children see. They are taught by example that it can be fun to be married— that it can be exciting to surprise each other. Who knows? Your little project might be passed down through generations.

Gifts say "I love you" and "I care." So give a gift to the one you love the very most.

Another time to spotlight your mate is on his birthday. I was intrigued with Carolyn's surprise birthday for her husband. As Marv was about to celebrate his fortieth birthday, she contacted his friends and both their families and gave each one a page from a scrapbook. She asked that they write down their recollections about Marv and give a page of memories as their gift to him, those pages to be compiled into a scrapbook.

Carolyn prepared a festive buffet. While the guests awaited Marv's arrival, they enjoyed nibbling and visiting. When the guest of honor opened the door, he was truly surprised to be greeted by a houseful of people, all shouting "Happy Birthday!" Carolyn seated Marv in the center of the guests and then she invited them to share their pages with him. Serious, warm memories were shared which caused a few tears. Funny moments brought laughter. Each page became a part of a huge scrapbook which, over the years, will still carry the same message: We love you, we care about you.

Sometimes we forget to plan special moments for our mates. We become deeply involved in building the self-esteem of our children, but how many times do we worry about building the self-esteem of our mates? No matter how young or how old, we all like to know that we are loved and are important to others.

One of the best projects to illustrate the good years which a husband and wife have shared is to create a book of memories. When Barry's "thirty-ninth and holding" birthday was approaching, I searched for a gift which could let him know how much our marriage meant to me. As I reflected upon the afternoon we met, the first date, the first Christmas card, I wanted to share those same warm memories with him. That was the beginning of my most exciting project—ever.

At the onset I didn't know exactly what the content would be. However, I did know that I must locate old calendars, journals, photo albums, and letters which might furnish clues to events of our fifteen years together. I mentioned my idea to our three older children, who were twelve, eleven, and nine at the time. As for the two tiny girls—well, I just hoped they would be understanding and give me the necessary time to compile the information. The older ones promised to help tend them after school, thus allowing me a little more time at the typewriter.

So the project began. I discovered a few pages which I had written previously about our first six years. What a find! That was all the motivation I needed. But after the first six years, I went through old calendars for important events. I had not always kept a journal faithfully, but I had kept our photo albums up to date and labeled. From the pictures came many memories as well as dates.

I called each of Barry's brothers and sisters, explained the venture, and asked if they would be a part of it, each writing a birthday wish to Barry and recalling on paper some shared memories. My "carrot" of encouragement was a dinner with all the trimmings which would be held the evening we presented the book. They all agreed.

His parents were next on the list. I was reluctant to ask both of them for letters; men are often hesitant about expressing themselves. But when Dad's letter came, I was thrilled to read this comment: "I am glad Karla asked me to write this letter to you on your birthday. This has caused me to reflect back over time and recall some of the happy experiences that have brought joy into our lives."

The amazing thing about compiling these books and asking people to write their memories is that they recall the happy times. The negative experiences tend to fade.

As Barry's father related those memorable moments, I was struck with the realization that these writing experiences exert a positive influence on the writers as well as the receivers.

Exciting anticipation preceded our adults-only dinner; the menu must wait while I wrote. The most pressing problem was locating information for the later years of our marriage.

Each morning before the older children left for school, they helped me straighten the house. When they ran out the door, I carried our little girls to the den and with the playpen and a stack of disposable diapers and crackers, we hibernated there. As I re-read the pages of rough draft, I had to chuckle when some of the sentences ended abruptly and then went on to other thoughts. No doubt that marked an occasion when one of the little girls had started to cry.

Each evening when Barry returned from work, he always inquired how my day had been. Occasionally, he asked what we had done. I tried to pretend nonchalance and hide my excitement. "Just the usual, Honey," I replied. "For some reason that keeps me pretty busy."

He always seemed satisfied with my answer. He had no idea what hectic days we were spending. One evening, however, I noticed him walk into the den. My heart skipped a beat; I had left in the typewriter some notes concerning our ninth year of marriage. I hoped he wouldn't notice it. I thought I heard him gasp. Oh, dear! I had forgotten to straighten the den before preparing dinner. There were still bottles and diapers, and the little girls' toys were scattered all over. I wondered if he would notice the calendars and journals strewn about the den. Fortunately, none of these matters seemed to catch his attention.

Completing a project as demanding as this one taught me the simple truth—that anything worthwhile requires effort. I am the first one to admit that I had to expend extra effort in order for my gift to materialize. But when the evening of the surprise party finally arrived, the early mornings at four and some of the late evenings which I had spent in organizing materials seemed worthwhile after all.

On his birthday all of Barry's brothers and sisters and their spouses arrived at our home, along with his parents, everyone grinning.

At 7:05 P.M. Barry arrived at home. As he opened the front door, we jumped out from behind counters and doors in the kitchen shouting, "Surprise!" And was he surprised!

We all gathered outside on the patio to enjoy our Mexican-style dinner in the warm September evening. After we were comfortably stuffed, we brought out a large gift-wrapped box for Barry, telling him it was our birthday gift. That gift seemed special to me because it was the product of one of my most valuable and limited possessions—my time.

When he lifted the binder out of the box and saw his picture framed on the outside, needless to say, he was amazed. As everyone gathered around to see the book, they all began laughing about some of the thoughts they had written and the memories they had recalled. Barry turned to his brothers' and sisters' letters, sharing aloud some of their comments. I hurriedly flipped on the tape recorder. These moments must be preserved. Story after story brought waves of laughter as we all shared our memories. Our sides were hurting and our jaws ached from laughing.

"Truly," Barry said, "What more could I ask for? Thank you for this special gift." He hugged each one as they left our home that evening, and I knew family bonds had been strengthened.

By the time his family left for home, our older children were in bed. Kelli and Kacee were still wide-eyed. I handed Barry his gift and told him to go upstairs and read the remainder of his book while the little girls and I cleaned up. A couple of hours later, after the girls were in bed and I had put the last few dishes into the cupboard, Barry sauntered down the stairs. I could tell he had spent some special moments reading my shared memories.

"You couldn't have given me anything nicer as a birthday gift," he said. "When the family was here and we read their pages, I think we all realized how much we love one another. And then tonight when I read the pages about our married years, I could hardly believe some of the moments you had recalled. How did you remember all those dates and events?"

I told him about the hectic two weeks of living in the den with the little girls while I searched albums and calendars and letters. "That's why our den was always so messy," I told him.

Then we took the book and together looked at our pages. "I knew we had grown over these last years," Barry said. "But when I saw it all in chronological order, including memories and not just dates and events, I came to realize how good our life together has really been." He gave me a warm hug, and then added, "You couldn't have ever given me a more priceless gift."

I knew I had given a gift which was already priceless to him, but would become a more and more valued treasure throughout the coming years. That book provided one of the best ways to share my deepest feelings for him. It truly said, "I love you."

Whether it be making a batch of fudge for your mate or trying to find a gift in the store—whether it be a note tucked under the pillow, or a book full of memories—caring about each other takes time and thought. But where could your time be better spent than in building your relationship with the one with whom you hope to spend eternity?

Take Time to Be a Parent

I recall Mother's statement of many years ago: "It was so much easier for my generation of women to be mothers. When we had children, it was naturally assumed that we would stay at home and rear them. But you poor modern mothers are stretched in many directions, usually away from your homes. If you choose to stay at home and be just a mother, you are ridiculed by society."

With all of the choices placed before us, it is difficult to know what is the best. That is why it is important that mothers communicate daily with their Heavenly Father. We need his guidance now more than ever before.

Elder Marvin J. Ashton stated, "Oh, how powerful are good women who choose the good part. . . . And although He will always be at our side if we will but invite Him, never will He take from His children the great gift of agency—the power to choose. Young mothers (single or otherwise) must learn to use this power wisely. There may be times when more than one course of action is placed before us. Each is right. It is then that wise and prudent decisions must be made, taking into consideration the season of life and the pertinent facts." ("Choose the Good Part," *Ensign,* May 1984, p. 9.)

When I talk with those whom I perceive as "super-moms" I am surprised to discover that many of them are struggling as hard as I am. Our imaginations tend to squelch realities. One example is when I spoke to some young mothers at a university, most of whom were helping their husbands get through college. As I walked into the room, I sensed immediately that several of them felt I could not offer much help because I could not relate with their situations. I was older than most of them, and they probably assumed that I had no little ones at home. The charming young woman who introduced me made me sound illustrious—and how can someone who lectures and writes books relate to someone who tends babies and cleans house?

After the introduction, feeling that I must break the barrier of superficiality, I said, "Wasn't that a grand introduction? So grand, in fact, that I have to admit that I don't know the person she introduced, even though she used my name." Laughter melted the barrier.

I proceeded to introduce them to the person standing before them. It was fun to share with them the fact that I had two preschoolers and another little one on the way. When I asked them if they could see the greenish tint in my cheeks, those young mothers who were also expecting breathed a sigh of recognition. Yes, other women experience that same dreadful sickness, also. With them I shared my memories as a young married woman helping her husband get through school. I shared the worries I had entertained that perhaps when he was out of school he might not locate a good job to his liking and capability. They needed to see someone who had walked in their footsteps and who had survived thus far. But the most special part of the evening was when I asked them to look at my well-worn hands.

"As I see other women's elegantly sculptured nails, I wonder if I will ever have the time to keep my hands in better condition. At present, they are in the dishwater and laundry too often for any hope. But I must let you know that I have discovered something much more exciting than sculptured nails, gorgeous wardrobes, or exotic cruises. The time spent with your husband and children is what life is all about."

I continued, "When you first saw me this evening, many of you questioned my ability to relate to your circumstances. All you saw was a woman who was dressed up and who didn't have babies crawling all over her lap and who had written a book. You might have even felt intimidated until you discovered that we have so much in common. We are both struggling to do our best. The only plus I have over you is that I am older, and hopefully those years have shed some understanding. I must let you know that if I had my life to live over, I would spend even more time with my husband and children, because at last I have begun to reap some of my rewards which are evidence that my efforts were not in vain.

"I have a teenage son," I told them, "who is the apple of my eye and we have so much fun joking and laughing with each other. He is tuned in to my feelings; he tries to help when he senses that I am experiencing a 'down.' I know that if I had not taken time with him when he was small, we would not be experiencing this good relationship now.

"I also have a daughter who means the world to me. In her young years we struggled to find a path together. It meant giving up luncheons with the ladies and taking her to lunch instead. Now as we run to the store to shop for school clothes, or as we sit visiting about life, I am most grateful for the bridge we took the time to build.

"And let me share just one more thought about another son. Barry and I waged a difficult battle to prove to him that he was every bit as important and outstanding as his older brother and sister. Now as I watch that young man participate in his sports, walking with confidence, there is nothing I would trade for all those hours invested with him in his younger days.

"Being able to reap some of the blessings of staying at home with our children makes me more determined than ever to spend my minutes, hours, and days with our little ones. The sculptured nails, the coiffured hair, the spotless clothes mean nothing when compared to one of your children."

Just as those young mothers first perceived me as a writer and speaker whose life must be full of exciting episodes, we often look at others and see only a small piece of the whole picture. Instead of comparing ourselves to others and what they seem to be accomplishing, we must chart our course and remember the seasons of our lives. Once our course is charted, we must set our goals accordingly.

"Set your goals," said Elder Ashton. "Without goals you can't measure your progress. But don't become frustrated because there are not obvious victories." ("Choose the Good Part," *Ensign,* May 1984, p. 11.)

For mothers with little ones at home, older children in school, and a husband with many responsibilities, times inevitably arise when a mother feels alone. You know you are loved by your children and husband, and yet you feel a heavy burden. Days full of appointments to the dentist, baseball practices, car repairs, PTA meetings, and church assignments are no respecters of a baby's naptime, housecleaning time, or meal preparation. Your head bursts with orders and invoices, and you are the only one who can fill them. What do you do at such times?

The easy advice is to get away and take time for yourself. But realistically that is not always possible, even though the experts tell us it is. *Some days require downright dog-biting grit to survive.* Those are the days when we come to grips with our inherent strengths.

I once heard the statement, "Strong mothers rear strong children. Weak mothers rear weak children." Of course, that is not always the case, but it is worth considering. Throughout the years my life has been blessed with great people who, each in his own way, helped me through many rough moments. Some gave me direct advice, some came to my aid, and others provided positive examples. As I pondered the love and admiration I felt for each one, it dawned on me that each of those women was sensitive and aware of others' needs and feelings. They were empathetic and charitable in the finest sense. But most interesting is that each one possessed determination and was a strong woman. While exercising great strength to overcome difficult moments, they had acquired the gifts of tenderness and caring. It was the combination of those two qualities which made them great.

When the weightlifter adds more pounds to the bar, he moans and groans as he initially lifts it. But he knows that if he never extends his efforts and keeps the weight below his ability, he will not gain new strength. However, the secret is to know how much he can handle. If he were to add too much weight and push himself beyond his limits, he could harm himself. However, he will never know without effort. President Spencer W. Kimball said it simply: "Lengthen your stride."

We must know ourselves, our needs, our dreams, our goals, and our limits. We must be wise enough to know how far we can push ourselves. The scriptures tell us that we will never be given greater trials or burdens than we can bear. We must converse with Heavenly Father and let him guide us. But we must *listen* to his advice because sometimes we buckle and complain when he adds more pounds to our bars. Instead of building strength, we let the bar fall to the ground.

The principle of taking the time to teach and guide children is paramount in my life. Yet every day the task grows more awesome; society inflicts strong negative pressures. As our children grow older, it is evident that their horizons need broadening; parents cannot provide all the experience they need. But to whom can we turn for assistance?

The summer Jeff turned fourteen and Scott eleven, we discussed an answer.

My brother, whose philosophy I have always admired, is a farmer. Since Kent lives in a rural area, we knew our boys could learn much from time spent with him. We live in the city, so he felt his girls (who are the same age as our boys) could broaden their horizons by learning something about our urban lifestyle. So we decided to trade two of our children for a week.

During our advance planning, Kent and I discussed desired areas of growth. I explained to Kent that Barry and I wanted our boys to learn about farming techniques, such as watering, weeding, and the operation of certain farm equipment. Some of my fondest memories at home were of early-morning weeding or working in the hay or the potatoes. I wanted my sons to share the experience. Kent said he would like his girls to learn new, different techniques of home management.

At first I was a little hesitant to have my nieces come to scrub walls. Even though Cori was their age and I could work with the three together, I was afraid they might resent coming to "work." When I expressed these concerns to Kent, we decided that we would explain to our children that they were not going on vacation but were going to work. I would pay his girls for their help and our boys would be Kent's hired hands.

Summer vacation finally arrived. We met halfway between both our homes and traded offspring. Of course, everyone was excited.

The minute the girls and I arrived home, we met for a briefing. I explained that every day we would learn some principle of home management. I also explained that they would be earning wages while they worked. We started with the concept of economy—saving work, time, and energy. Then we grabbed pails and cloths and started washing down the walls in the hallways. I let them turn on the portable radio full blast with their kind of music. I wanted them to understand that even though there are always unpleasant tasks waiting to be done in a home, there are ways of combating drudgery. One is to work with music.

That evening after dinner, they recorded in their journals what they had learned that day. I also reminded them that the next day, Tuesday, we would scrub bathrooms. I laughed at their moans and groans.

On Tuesday, they worked hard, but it was evident they needed a lift. I cornered Kim and Cori and asked if they would like to plan a surprise party for Cheri, since her birthday was near. That's all it took. Amid the cleaning of counters and drawers, the two girls whispered plans back and forth. That evening we had a great party which provided the motivation to keep them going. Again, they recorded the day's events in their journals.

Wednesday found them not very excited about organizing and working in the kitchen. They cleaned and arranged cupboards, not only for attractiveness, but for improved convenience. They scrubbed and scrubbed. By afternoon, not even the music seemed to ease their tiredness. I asked who would like to go to the waterslide. They all cheered. The kitchen was finished in a hurry.

That afternoon we tackled another project which they really enjoyed. The night before, I had taken the girls to the store to purchase any item which they felt could be used in tending children. I explained that whenever they were tending children, whether their own little brothers and sisters or the neighbors, instead of just watching the children, they were also to teach them. For the afternoon they were assigned to teach Kelli and Kacee. I left. They were in full charge.

When I returned late in the afternoon, they were eager to show me all they had done with the little girls. They had created puppets, pretzel butterflies, flowers, and yarn dolls with sucker heads, as well as doing the more usual activities such as coloring. Impressed with their creative efforts, I challenged them to always retain the "teach and tend" concept so that someday, when they are mothers, they will teach their own children and not just watch them grow.

On Thursday, they enjoyed planning good, nutritious meals for the family. They planned a menu of turkey, potatoes, gravy, Grandma's good dressing, rolls, salad, and a mint dessert. They also were in charge of setting an attractive table, complete with candlelight. As evening approached, they thoroughly enjoyed serving their meal. They recorded that day's experiences in detail in their journals.

I had scheduled Friday as a shopping day in which the girls could learn wise purchasing techniques. After straightening the house, we were off to the stores, just browsing and searching for school needs. Then we went sightseeing. As we left the mall and entered the busy streets, Kimberly grabbed my hand.

"I don't know if I like the city," she said, tightly clutching my hand. "It's so noisy—it kind of scares me."

We visited Barry's office. Obviously the girls were intrigued by the fact that every day Barry drove into a large city where he worked in his office; his job was quite different from their father's work. Barry took us to lunch, after which we continued shopping. That evening we showed Barry our purchases and shared with him our exciting day.

For their journals I had copied pages reminding the girls of some of the things we had learned and worked on. Then I wrote them each a note, telling them how special it had been to have them with us for that week. As they closed their journals, it was evident the week had been monumental to them. I felt doubly grateful for this trading project. During those days, not only had I gotten help with major household tasks, but I had also come to know my nieces better and to appreciate their unique qualities.

Saturday, our two families met at the halfway mark. We were eager to reclaim our boys.

"How do you like farming?" was my first question. I doubt that our sons want to be farmers—but they had some exciting stories to tell. We gathered at a nearby park to compare notes and share stories before returning to our respective homes.

Just before leaving, Kent handed me an envelope. Inside were his journal accounts of the week with Jeff and Scott. He had written about each day's events. As we drove toward Bountiful, I read the journal entries aloud. Then I was instructed to hand each one a personal envelope. Inside Kent had listed ten reasons each one had earned a bonus, and then he had included their paychecks.

The project was more successful than either family anticipated. We each more fully understood and loved our nieces and nephews, and their horizons had been broadened.

One of the finest lessons we can teach our young children is how to relate not only to other people in the world, but also to their animal friends. We are fortunate to have many natural "pets" in our backyard for the children to observe. One cold February morning with seven inches of new snow on the ground, Kelli and Kacee ran to the window and squealed when they spotted their pet squirrel coming to eat the bread crumbs they had thrown out. As he nibbled the bread, his bushy tail was snug on his back, and it looked like a thick fur blanket around him.

"Mom, maybe he's cold," Kelli said. "Can he come in the house with us?"

Here was an opportunity to explain how Mother Nature provides animals with coats of fur to keep them warm during winter months. We watched the little squirrel jump high into one of the trees.

"Just think," I told Kelli and Kacee, "You're so lucky to have a pet you can feed and care for, and yet he's free to do the things he loves."

"But what does 'free' mean?" Kelli queried.

"Remember when Scotty tied you to the bed and you couldn't get loose?" I asked. Kelli nodded. "Well," I continued, "When some people want a squirrel for a pet, they have to catch one and imprison it inside a pen or cage. Then the little animal is not free. He feels like you did when you couldn't get loose from Scott's bed. He can't run to all the places he wants to investigate. You're free just like your pet squirrel. No one is tying you down and making you stop learning."

Of course there was much more that could have been said. But she started to wriggle, and I could sense that she had learned quite enough for one moment. She wanted to be "free" and run back to the window to watch her pet.

Another phase of learning pertains to teaching children about their relationship with older people. For example, a dear neighbor suffers from a serious heart condition. At first the little girls were very shy when we visited her, taking a loaf of bread or some other goody. But before long they anticipated our walks down the road. Whenever they helped me bake cookies or brownies, often Kelli said, "We need to take some to Mrs. Coleman."

She was learning her lesson well. Mrs. Coleman adored those two little characters. She longed to reach out and hug and kiss them. But they had not overcome their shyness yet. So she backed off and continued to be content with a good-bye and a smile.

One day when we baked cookies, Kelli grabbed a plate

and said, "Let's take cookies to Mrs. Coleman." With Kacee, we were on our way, Kelli carrying the cookies and Kacee bundled in my arms.

Kelli rang the doorbell and grinned as Ruth answered. "Hi," Kelli said, in her childlike, shy way. Kacee grinned.

After a delightful visit, we put on our coats. Without prompting, Kelli ran up to Ruth and gave her a big hug and kiss. "I love you," she whispered softly.

"And I love you, too, Kelli," said our dear friend. "Oh, Karla, how I've waited for this moment. There's nothing like the love of a little child." She gave Kacee a big hug and kiss, and Kacee waved her enthusiastic "bye-bye," which she had recently mastered.

As we skipped home, Kelli was trying to balance herself on a railroad tie which outlined our neighbor's yard. She stopped abruptly and said, "Mom, I love Mrs. Coleman. I love you. I love my baby. I love the *whole* world!"

"Kelli," I said, kneeling down to her pint-size stature. "You made Mrs. Coleman happy today because you told her you love her. Isn't it nice to make people happy? Don't you feel good inside?" She nodded. "I sure do love you," I told her.

She was learning.

Often we hear the statement, "You can't love others until you love yourself." I contend that you cannot fully love yourself until you love others. The two concepts are intertwined. Kelli was exploring self-discovery, but only when she began extending her love to those around her could she begin to say, "I love everybody and everybody loves me."

If we want our time to count with our children, we must be on the same wave length. Their grades might be good, and their sports and other activities might seem to be fine, also. However, my father taught me an important concept when he told me to look into the children's eyes to learn of their inner welfare.

I have tried to follow his advice, even though I realize problems are not always so easily detected. However, many times when I have earnestly looked into our children's eyes while they are talking, I have sensed trouble. That is my first signal.

Not long ago, I looked into our Scott's eyes. His reluctance to look me in the eye aroused my concern. Immediately I began recalling his actions during the past few weeks. There were indications that all was not well within.

Cori had been taking a great deal of our time with her drill competitions, and many of our family conversations centered on her activities. Jeff had also been achieving in his Scouting and we had often voiced our enthusiasm over his becoming an Eagle when he turned thirteen. Of course, it seemed we were always making a fuss over the little girls and their continuing antics.

Who was left out? Scotty. Being the middle child is sometimes difficult. I'll always recall with fondness one evening when Scott was feeling low. As we sat chatting before bedtime, I told him the story about Rob, my brother, and how he felt it was terrible to be the middle child because he was always being ignored. Scott's eyes lit up and he said, "I know how he felt." Then he continued to share his feelings about being the middle child.

But before he could drown in his self-pity, I said, "Always remember, Scott, whenever things seem a little difficult, there are more blessings in store. First of all, you are not only our middle child, but you are also the third child. Do you realize that three is a lucky number? *You* are that lucky child. No matter how long you live or how many children we have, you will always be number three—the lucky one.

"You've been lucky from day one," I continued. "You

were our first baby to be born without any problems at birth, and you were born with a happy disposition. You've made lots of friends right from the beginning and everybody always liked you. You might be the middle one, but you are certainly the lucky one. And whenever you start feeling down, then just remember your lucky number."

Amazingly, his spirits were rejuvenated. His eyes sparkled.

A couple of days later when he and Jeff were arguing, he blurted out in defense, "That's okay. I'm number three!"

Of course, Jeff did not realize the implication and had no retort. But Scott beamed.

However, that particular night as we sat on his bed, I could sense a deeper feeling of despair—so listening became the medicine.

Sunday morning we were all preparing for church when Scott ran down the stairs, his tousled blond hair sticking straight up in front. I couldn't help laughing, even though I knew I should have restrained myself. Before he could manage his hurt feelings, I rushed him into the bathroom and grabbed the curling iron.

"No way, Mom, you're not using that on me! Only girls curl their hair," he objected.

"Oh, no, they don't," called Cori from the kitchen. "Even our cousin uses a curling iron to make his hair feather."

"But Jeff doesn't have to use a curling iron," Scott added.

"Jeff is probably one in a million whose hair will naturally feather," I said. (Of course I had to exaggerate a little to make my point.)

Jeff shouted from the stairs, "Come on, Scott. Let Mom use the iron."

Soon everyone had gathered in the bathroom, absorbed in the feathering job on Scott's hair. Of course he had to act somewhat irritated at everyone hovering over him, telling me where to curl next. But it was good for him to have all that attention. When we finished the feathering, Cori looked at Scott and gave him one of those modern gestures which denoted how "tough" he looked. And Jeff agreed, "You look great, Scott." Even Kelli had to tell Scotty how "neat" he looked.

By the time we left for church, Scott was grinning and his eyes were sparkling. However, in order for his continued self-esteem to flourish, we all knew we needed to continue our visible show of concern and love for him. So we all decided it was time to help Scott work on his Bear award in Cub Scouting. His reluctance to work on his projects soon disappeared. Love performs miracles.

One evening as I was preparing dinner, Scott was planning to complete a project but he could see that I was busy peeling vegetables. So he closed his book. At that moment Jeff came along and asked him what he had left to do. Scott showed him, and Jeff (bless his caring soul) said, "Oh, that's easy. Since I'm older, I can pass you off on the requirement." So the two of them sat at the counter, Jeff tutoring and Scott memorizing; before we knew it, he had completed part of the project.

"But I still have to build something," Scott said in despair.

"Oh, that's easy too, Scott," Jeff said, taking the book. "Come on, let's go downstairs and build something together."

At the counter sink, tears ran down my cheeks — and I wasn't even peeling onions.

Another "perspective idea" I gleaned from my father was to look at the child's facial expression in photos. Of course, occasionally every child is in a bad mood. But study the expressions over several different picture-taking episodes. They certainly tell a lot about a child's feelings. Those facial expressions indicate when he needs individual attention.

One way to build a child's self-esteem is to help him realize that he is an important part of a vital group — his family. One family project which helps to bond family members as well as to build individual self-esteem is collecting pictures of shared moments throughout the year. At year's end, from the photo album extract ten or more pictures of memorable events and make them into a picture collage. Create an annual picture collage, using school pictures as well as snapshots of memorable occasions. Date the mat. This is a simple way to record in visual form shared moments of family events and physical development during a particular year.

Use the same idea with one of the outstanding events of the children. The summer in which Scott's baseball team took first place in the state, I did a picture collage for him to hang in his bedroom. In the fall this was his birthday gift. Someday he will enjoy recalling that year with his own son.

Another family bond builder is just plain talking with each other. Whether it be at Sunday dinner, early breakfast, after school — whenever — just talk.

Our neighbors, whose children are now gone, cautioned us to allow our children, especially those in teen years, to voice their own opinions, even though they might differ from the parents' view. Children need assurance that their ideas are valid and will be respected in the family circle.

By talking together, parents can more easily put themselves in the child's situation. For example, one afternoon Scott brought a friend home. I was disgusted with Scott for not following through on an assignment and I scolded him right in front of his peer. In the privacy of the hallway Scott said to me, "Why do you have to embarrass me in front of my friend?"

My cheeks reddened. He was absolutely right. I apologized and agreed that if he had done that to me, I would have been as embarrassed as he. It was a learning experience for me. But had Scott and I not been able to voice our feelings to each other, he might still be harboring ill feelings over that episode.

Taking time to talk with our children should begin at an early age. Poor Kelli. When she turned two, a new baby entered our home—and from the beginning, Kacee had the energy of a wind-up toy which never runs down. She was constantly on the move and into a mess. Kelli noticed that as I chased Kacee from mess to mess, I often tried to shift her attention to a worthwhile project by laughing with her and tickling her. Kelli caught the message. Make a mess and Mom will notice and play with you. She sidled up to me and asked in her quiet voice, "Mom, can I be your baby?"

Another baby like Kacee I didn't need at that moment, but I readily sensed her feelings. "Of course you can be my baby," I said. "But how I'll miss having my big girl around. You see, Honey, I love to talk with my big girl and I love to have someone who can put puzzles together and someone who can sing songs with me."

Kelli crawled into my arms. "I want to be your baby."

So I wrapped her in her favorite blanket and told her a story about that certain blanket. Then I cuddled her in my arms and reassured her that if she wanted to be my baby, she could. However, I explained, "Be sure and let me know when you want to be my big girl again, because I'll miss having her around."

Kelli smiled and sat in my arms as I rocked her. For the remainder of the day, she often told me that she was still my baby. After letting her join in the messes with her baby sister and after an almost nightmarish day, I wondered if I had done the right thing by going along with her whim. But the following day I knew the answer. After breakfast and some games, as I was mopping up the juice which Kacee had thrown all over the floor, Kelli approached me. She put her arm around my neck and looked into my eyes. "I'm not a baby any more, Mom. Now I'm a big girl."

"Hooray," I shouted, grabbing her. "I'm so glad to have my big girl back, because I surely do need her help."

Another way to improve parenting skills is to have an evaluation. Who are the best candidates to assist in this evaluation? Your children.

With older children, you might give them sheets of paper and have them list anonymously three items they like about you. Then have each of them list one thing he would like you to change.

Even little ones can be of great help. Sometimes their genuine honesty stings for a moment, but those initial jolts initiate action. When one little five-year-old was asked to name three things she liked about her mother, she replied, "I like when she buys me shoes. I like when she makes me clothes. I like when she takes me to the store."

When another five-year-old was asked, she said, "I like when she makes me treats. I love the way she loves me. I like when she reads me stories."

Those five-year-olds told a great deal in their answers.

With the small children, seize an opportune moment to sit down and look into their eyes and ask them to tell you what they like about you. Then ask if there is anything they don't like. When asked what she didn't like about Mom, my little three-year-old answered, "I know you're mad when you have a frowny face and I don't like you to have a frowny face."

I learned a lesson from her. Following her comments, I have consciously worked at maintaining a pleasant countenance.

Another way of evaluating techniques is to read between the lines of any notes or letters received from your children. When our older children were younger, they were eager to share their journal entries with me, and many times those between-the-lines messages suggested areas where I needed improvement.

In order to take self-evaluations seriously, you must be hardy and not succumb to feelings of inadequacy or self-condemnation. Remember, improvement is the reason behind the evaluation. By all means you must realize that many of the things you do are appreciated and liked by your children. I'll always cherish a letter from Scott, our eleven-year-old. On Mother's Day he expressed in writing his appreciation for some of the things I do for him. But the line which caught my eye was, "Especially I like that you are a house mom. A lot of kids don't have a mom around the house all the time who can go to their games and do things for them."

A house mom! I'd like that engraved on my tomb-stone. In fact, that little phrase meant so much to me that the following day when I registered Kelli for kindergarten, on the blanks listing mother's occupation I wrote "house mom." Even moms who stay at home can still feel impor-tant with such a title and recognition.

But whether a house mom or a working mom, if our time is to really count, we must try not to hurry it. No doubt professional child psychologists might have had a better approach than mine. But if I want my time to really count, then I must stay in tune, in order to receive advice from the One who knows the best answers. Sometimes I can't explain what I do when our children need my extra effort, but I do know that if I am in harmony, then I receive workable solutions. Staying in tune is worth the effort because of the help received.

One fall, after the older children left for their first day of school, I shared with Kelli (who was three) and Kacee (who was one) my excitement about projects with them during the coming nine months. Of course they could not fully comprehend all that I told them, but they seemed to grasp my enthusiasm.

One of the first projects we worked on was "Learning About Me." I had heard a psychologist say that the first three years of life is the time to establish a good self-image. His ideas were intriguing and made sense. Therefore, this project was intended to help our little girls know what special people they are.

One afternoon we were at the grocery store when a child about the age of Kelli ran to our cart and stood staring at the little girls. I noticed her looking at the big red bows tied around their ponytails. She ran to find her mother, wanting to show her the bows. The mother seemed almost as intrigued as her little daughter.

"Your girls look like picture dolls," the mother commented. Then she grabbed her little girl's hand and said, "Come on, Kathy. You'll just have to be my little tomboy."

All the rest of the day I couldn't forget that brown-eyed child who would have looked just like a "picture doll" if her long brown hair had been tied with a bow. That incident was an inspiration. If our little girls were to feel good about themselves, they needed reassurance that they were unique. And bows and ribbons in a little girl's hair is like the finishing touch on a special package.

Each morning we took time to neatly comb, braid, or curl the little girls' hair and tied on bows. I could not believe the comments from total strangers as we went about our usual tasks of shopping at the market or even taking their older sister to drill practices. The girls received positive praise. While we were purchasing some light bulbs, a lady stopped and smiled at the girls. She patted their soft pink cheeks.

"My, you cute little dolls. You make me think of my granddaughter who lives far away from me." She then turned to me and said, "You're so lucky."

"Mom," said Kelli. "That lady really likes me and baby."

Again, those magical bows had initiated another moment of building the girls' self-esteem. When people commented and stopped to give them a pat or hug, the message was, "They like me."

Yes, it takes a little extra time to tie bows and comb hair. But anything worthwhile takes effort. My effort paid off tenfold.

Also, whenever young children are clean and attractive, they are like magnets attracting people who cannot resist giving hugs and pats. Here again, keeping those little fingers clean and those little soft cheeks free from smudges is often a task, but is worth the effort.

One evening when our family gathered for family home evening, Kelli was in charge of the program. She led the family in the song, "I Am a Child of God" and then she presented the thought. She looked at all of us and said simply, "I love everybody. It's fun to be a family." A sermonette!

Such lessons are absorbed from the very beginning. In reality, we are accomplishing a great deal even though we may feel that everyday moments are insignificant. As I was hurrying to straighten our home one morning, Kacee, who was a small baby then, started to cry and fuss.

"Not already," I thought to myself. It seemed as though I had just fed her. But as we cuddled in the rocker, time stood still. I was reminded that I held a precious gift.

With each of our children, I have learned that feeding time is a nourishing time, not only for the body, but also for the mind. And it does as much good for the mother's soul as for the baby's. This is a perfect time to contemplate the blessings of the day. With a baby in one's arms, it's easy to recognize true blessings. If there is one word of advice for young mothers with babies, I would tell them never to pass up those moments of feeding time. Often they interrupt important projects, but past experience has taught me that very few things rank with the importance of cuddling and feeding infants. Ignore the urge to prop the bottle and let the little one lie in bed and eat. Yes, he will receive his food, but his needs are much greater. He needs to be cuddled and hugged and reassured.

The nursing mother must take the time to sit down and feed her baby. But the temptation to prop a bottle seems to come when the mother stops nursing or when she

bottle-feeds her baby from the beginning. Granted, sometimes we feel as if we can't move another exhausted
muscle, and those moments often come with middle-of-
the-night feedings. With a little more effort, however, those
early-morning feedings can become some of the choicest
moments spent with children.

I recall hearing a mother share these thoughts: "As I
sat and nursed my babies, I talked to them in whispers and
shared with them the desires of my heart. If I was bothered
or saddened, I told them of my feelings. Or I shared my
exuberance. Many times I told them quietly of my deep
love for them. Sometimes I quietly opened my scriptures
and read to them.

"As my children grew older and those moments faded,
I realized that I had gained a great deal. I had always experienced a closeness to each one of our children. And when I
saw them grow to love the scriptures, I recalled our
moments spent together in the rocking chair during their
infancy. I'm grateful for hungry tummies which provided
moments to begin our mother-child relationship. As a
result, we have always been able to share our feelings,
whether in sorrow or joy."

Those moments of sharing feelings are invaluable for
both parent and child. I overheard a mother telling another
that she had to get out of the house because she was bored.
Her remark was, "You can speak to children only so long."

My heart sank. She had given up too early! What child
cannot learn from a parent? What parent cannot learn from
a child? Children teach us to regenerate optimism. They
teach us to love the simple. They teach us to spot the
unique and beautiful. They remind us what love is all
about. Yes, children are natural teachers from whom
parents can learn.

Just as the sculptor must take sufficient time to mold
his creation, in many respects the parent has a hand in
molding his live clay. We can only do this by spending time
on the children. In our fast-paced society, we scurry from

one appointment to another. Our schedules are tight, which leaves us little space to receive inspiration to stir our souls. But it is not always important to accomplish many tasks during the day. What counts is touching people around us.

Whether we like it or not, we are teachers to those young people who have come to live with us. By our thoughts, words, and actions, we are teaching them patience or impatience, love or dislike, compassion or apathy.

The following poem says it:

> I took a piece of plastic clay
> And idly fashioned it one day,
> And as my fingers pressed it still
> It moved and yielded to my will.
>
> I came again when days were past—
> The bit of clay was hard at last;
> The form I gave it, it still bore,
> But I could change that form no more.
>
> I took a piece of living clay
> And gently formed it day by day,
> And molded with my power and art
> A young child's soft and yielding heart.
>
> I came again when years were gone—
> It was a man I looked upon;
> He still that early impress wore,
> And I could change him nevermore.
>
> —Author unknown

I hope you do not interpret these pages as meaning that I think I have mastered parenting. Each day brings new problems to solve and new, bewildering situations. Sometimes I am concerned that I do not share enough of the everyday situations which illustrate our own family's need for constant improvement.

For example, I have had several people ask, "Is your home always spotless?" My immediate response is, "Absolutely not!" With several children who have individual and varied ambitions and dreams, and with a busy, involved husband, I find myself overloaded with the usual carpools and appointments, not to mention the full-time task of keeping our home in order. Therefore, not every corner is sparkling and dust-free, and not every room is clutter-free. However, I have learned a great deal over the last few years. At first I believed that if I taught the children to put their toys and clothes in a designated area, that would take care of the clutter. Reality has taught that there is a certain amount of clutter and chaos just by having a number of bodies circulating in the same area.

We must allow ample space for each individual. If we have several children, space is at a premium. However, if the mother is expected to allow space for the children, then her feelings must also be respected. When children are very young, they should be taught that mother is not a slave. If there is work to be done, everyone available should be involved.

One management trick has succeeded in our home. Before the older children leave for school, they each have at least one cleaning chore to complete. Those mornings I let them slip out the door without doing their chores remind me of how much their efforts help. Also, each family member is responsible for keeping his own bedroom in order. If the bedrooms are tidy, coupled with three major jobs completed (one for each school-age child), I am not overwhelmed with chores early in the morning.

It is important for the whole family to discuss the household chores and agree on how to handle them. Nagging doesn't work. Therefore, I use a worksheet which places responsibility where it belongs—fairly with each child. Expect them to do their jobs well, then respect their efforts. Approach household chores with a positive atti-

Worksheet

On Monday I:
- ☐ Made my bed
- ☐ Picked up my clothes
- ☐ Brushed my teeth
- ☐ Practiced the piano or worked on Scouting
- ☐ Did one job which needed to be done in the house
- ☐ Did one job for Mom

On Tuesday I:
- ☐ Made my bed
- ☐ Picked up my clothes
- ☐ Brushed my teeth
- ☐ Practiced the piano or worked on Scouting
- ☐ Did one job which needed to be done in the house
- ☐ Did one job for Mom

On Wednesday I:
- ☐ Made my bed
- ☐ Picked up my clothes
- ☐ Brushed my teeth
- ☐ Practiced the piano or worked on Scouting
- ☐ Did one job which needed to be done in the house
- ☐ Did one job for Mom

On Thursday I:
- ☐ Made my bed
- ☐ Picked up my clothes
- ☐ Brushed my teeth
- ☐ Practiced the piano or worked on Scouting
- ☐ Did one job which needed to be done in the house
- ☐ Did one job for Mom

On Friday I:
- ☐ Made my bed
- ☐ Picked up my clothes
- ☐ Brushed my teeth
- ☐ Practiced the piano or worked on Scouting
- ☐ Did one job which needed to be done in the house
- ☐ Did one job for Mom

On Saturday I:
- ☐ Made my bed
- ☐ Cleaned my room and closet
- ☐ Cleaned one room in the house other than my room
- ☐ Did three jobs for Mom

On Sunday I:
- ☐ Rested from my labors!!!

Name _____

Owe $ _____

tude. I have discovered that if I am excited and encourage the children to hurry and get the work done, we all work a little faster. Included is the worksheet which I am using at present. At the week's end, we settle on allowances; they earn a full or part allowance according to the number of accomplishments on their sheets.

Of course, we have not always used this particular worksheet. For the present, however, it works well for us. When the children were younger, we used many different types. Worksheets or working arrangements should be unique, depending on a family's needs.

Just as each family's needs are unique, so are the discoveries waiting under the stacks of dirty clothes or of clean clothes to be folded, around floors waiting to be mopped, and behind meals waiting to be prepared.

Take time to savor the simple incidents which increase our understanding of life as a parent. One afternoon I was in the mall shopping with the two little girls. Kelli was tired and she crawled into the stroller, wanting to be pushed. With packages in my hand, I let go of the handles. Instantly two-year-old Kacee grabbed them. She too was getting tired, and since she could not ride in the stroller, she was determined to push it. As she turned the stroller toward the escalator, I put my hand on hers and turned it the other way. She threw herself on the floor and let out a yell.

I turned to see a distinguished gray-haired gentleman watching us. He sauntered to my side and said, "I've been watching you with your little girls." I felt my heart skip a beat. I secretly wondered if he were going to give me a lecture on how to handle ill-mannered children. But he continued, "I'm from Chicago and I'm visiting here with family. When I saw you with your little girls, I recalled some of the memories I have, being a father. When your little girl threw herself on the floor, she reminded me of my son. My, he was quite a boy. But I now understand that children with all that determination grow into great people. That little girl will certainly amount to something someday."

I'm sure that observant gentleman didn't mean to give me a bundle of wisdom that day, but he surely did. As he turned to leave, he said, with a twinkle in his eye, "God bless you."

All the way home his words rang in my ears and in my heart. At day's end my little ones were tired, my own body was weary just from chasing them, and I still had dinner to prepare and an almost endless list of other chores. Nevertheless, the man's wise words buoyed me up. "Yes," I mused." "God bless us mothers everywhere."

P.S.

During the last nine months of the two years of writing this book, I was expecting our sixth baby. As I lived frustrations, fears, and sometimes negative feelings, I shared them throughout these pages. Certainly I could never relate something I had not experienced.

Now as I cuddle my newborn, I have no doubts that the traumas and fears prepared me for the insurmountable joy of once again being a new mother.

My days are filled with changing diapers, washing, feeding, and bathing our baby Kristy as well as mothering our two other preschoolers. It seems I hardly find time for a shower before the older children rush in from school — and it's time for dinner. Instead of feeling bored, as I once feared, I find life full and rewarding.

Being an older new mother has many hidden golden moments. I recognize the fact that far too soon my newborn will be running out the door to kindergarten. My oldest teenager will be at home only a few more years before leaving to begin his journey in life. Consequently, more than ever, I am compelled to take the time with Barry and each one of our children, for now I understand more fully how short is our stay here on earth.

My senses have been heightened. Hearing our baby's first cry in the delivery room brought back a flood of memories of when we first met each one of our other children.

My actions and reactions are repeated for the sixth time:

> Cupping my newborn's miniature head in my hand,
> Watching her fingers clutch tightly around one of
>   mine,
> Looking into her eyes and wondering what her
>   thoughts are,
> Holding her close while I feed her,
> Tucking her into that same bassinet her brothers
>   and sisters all slept in,
> Watching our older children begin a new
>   relationship with their infant sister,
> Catching glimpses of Barry picking her up and
>   talking to her as only a father can to a new
>   daughter.

I must admit that the sixth time has heightened those simple moments. Never have I felt so compelled to make my time count, for I know I have only begun to appreciate and understand the magnitude of my calling as a wife and mother.

Take Time To Measure Progress

Many years ago, when I left my professional career to begin my new career of being a "house mom," I never dreamed of the adventures that lay ahead. At present, I am in the midst of that adventure. My days are filled with the usual tasks of caring for our children, preparing meals, cleaning, washing, fulfilling church callings, helping neighbors in need, and so on. There are no cymbals clanging or fireworks lighting the sky to assure me that I'm doing a good job. But there are simple moments each day which reaffirm the fact that I'm on the right track.

Sometimes I become impatient and desire the pot of gold before the rainbow ends. Those are the times when advice is necessary, such as Elder Marvin J. Ashton's. He admonished, "Remind yourself that striving can be more important than arriving. If you are striving for excellence —if you are trying your best, day by day, with the wisest use of your time and energy to reach realistic goals—you are a success." ("Choose the Good Part," *Ensign,* May, 1984, p. 11.)

When just a sophomore in high school, I sat at my desk watching the second hand on the huge wall clock tick away each minute. Time dragged as I eagerly awaited the bell. But all too suddenly those seconds became years, and now our oldest son is a sophomore in high school, watching a clock and waiting for the bell to ring.

Throughout my young life I was forced to climb many foothills which gradually prepared me for the oncoming mountains to be scaled. Ahead lie still more rugged and jagged peaks, waiting to test my strength and endurance. I am grateful for the green meadows in life, for it is often while resting from the arduous climb that I can measure my progress and try to answer the question, "Am I taking the time to make my time count?"